CHANGE IS.

Change Is.
Valued

Management education and leadership development are, like most other aspects of modern life, undergoing a revolution – what we have been doing is not working. Not only must we seek new ideas, solutions, and concepts of leadership but we must teach them in revolutionary ways. The myth and the fable are examples of the powerful means of education which have slipped into disuse these days. Stephen Baetz brings back the tradition of storytelling in the thoughtful tale he has woven about personal and organizational change. *Change Is.* will stir your imagination, stimulate the neurons, and call you to action.
Dr. Lance H.K. Secretan
AUTHOR, THE WAY OF THE TIGER

With the amount and velocity of change facing us in the next decade, we'd all benefit from a meeting place like the attic and the understanding of an Abernathy and friends. The Wasiswill Codes and their process of self-discovery is a model we could well use to help us grow and adapt to the times ahead.
Jack Speake
EXECUTIVE VICE PRESIDENT (RETIRED), CANADA TRUST

Enjoy becoming a part of change in your organization. Stephen Baetz brings organizational change and human behavioural insights to a high art in this thoroughly enjoyable tale.
Eric Daly
VICE PRESIDENT INFORMATION SERVICES, ROYAL LEPAGE

Change process is an inside out approach. One's core paradox acts as a guide if one listens to the silence of one's thoughts.
Fred Mathewson
MANAGER, THE WOODBRIDGE GROUP

Change, how to implement it, and its possible effects described not in the typical, intimidating, high brow fashion but instead in an informative and easy-to-read parable. I enjoyed reading a management book – *for a change!*
Dave Chilton
AUTHOR, THE WEALTHY BARBER

Change Is. should be read and re-read, not only by corporate Vice Presidents of Planning, but also by line Supervisors, Spouses, Parents, and anyone else seeking to improve the world in which they live and/or work.
Cal Swegles
MANAGER EMPLOYMENT SERVICES AND TRAINING,
UNIVERSITY OF GUELPH

An entertaining guide to organizational change – full of humour and common sense that our organization has come to associate with Stephen Baetz.
Mary Ellen Selby
SUPERVISOR TRAINING AND EMPLOYMENT,
HOME OIL COMPANY LTD.

This is a critical work with messages for all companies desiring to succeed in the next century. For a company like First Echo Group, that is in business to enact the vision, Stephen's book is required reading for all managers.
Paul Motz
PRESIDENT, FIRST ECHO GROUP

Stephen, the book is just like you ... philosophical, creative, funny, and involving. It inspires a fearless approach to change. Norcen has been rewarded by your work.
Karen Behar
SUPERVISOR RECRUITMENT AND STAFF DEVELOPMENT,
NORCEN ENERGY LIMITED

Must reading for senior managers assessing or reassessing the need for strategic planning and management education within their organizations. It is also a splendid introductory reading for managers about to participate in management education programs.
Hugh W. Sloan, Jr.
PRESIDENT, WOODBRIDGE AUTOMOTIVE GROUP

CHANGE IS.

A PERSONAL GUIDE
FOR ORGANIZATIONAL CHANGE

STEPHEN BAETZ

Charles Nathan Publishing

ISBN 1-895402-00-X
Published in 1991 by
Charles Nathan Publishing
A Division of LIVE Consultants Inc.
46 King Street South
St. Jacobs, Ontario
Canada
N0B 2N0
(519) 664-1333

Canadian Cataloguing in Publication Data

Baetz, Stephen, 1948–

Change is. : a personal guide for organizational change

ISBN 1-895402-00-X

1. Organizational change. 2. Change (Psychology).
3. Management – Psychological aspects. I. Title.

HD58.8.B34 1991   658.4'06   C90-095891-X

Book Design: jg publishing services inc.
Illustration: Marion Woeller
Printed and bound in Canada by John Deyell Company

Table of Contents

Acknowledgements

WHEN I WAS IN HIGH SCHOOL, an English teacher made the observation that everyone we meet becomes a part of us. At that age and stage in my life, I rejected the idea. Perhaps the struggle for individuality didn't allow me to see how connected we all are.

Much experience later, I understand the truth in the message: everyone we meet becomes a collaborative partner in shaping our understanding and insight.

Change Is. is truly a collaboration. It has been shaped by numerous people I know personally as well as individuals I know only by what they have written or said. Hoot has an ability I wish I had – she can remember who said what. Much of what has been given to me and is reflected in this book didn't come with a tag that gave credit to the source. For missing the chance to offer due credit, I apologize.

There are many people, however, whose witting and unwitting collaboration I value.

Marilyn has been not only a wise business partner but also a caring and strong life-partner. She listened to each and every draft and, as always, provided straight, honest feedback. The years have taught me to trust her instincts, her wisdom, and her judgement.

I have been lucky enough to work with a team of people within LIVE Consultants Inc. who live the values that are important to us and to our clients. They work hard to deliver quality on time and that has always impressed me. I am grateful for the solid support of Gary Bond, Geoff Bowden, Jani Corbett, Art Dayman, Chris Diesbourg, Lori McNulty, Colleen Shoemaker, and Joyce Widmeyer.

Of course, many of the ideas have been shaped by dialogue and discussions that I have had with seminar participants and with clients. The problems and opportunities that they face have helped to provide clarity since they require and demand practical responses.

There are many others who are part of this book, whether they are aware of it or not: my parents who taught me the important paradox of thoughtful action. Fred Mathewson, who impresses me with his desire to do the right thing. Jack Speake, who asks me to stand on my head to gain a new perspective. Aarne Siirala, who taught me that questions are more important than answers. Don Deverall and Dennis Eaton, who encourage me to teach by story and example. Paul Motz, who is thoughtful.

Others have touched me by what they have written. They have allowed me to be their dialogue partners. I read eclectically. Dennis Lee, Robert Munsch, Mordecai Richler, W.O. Mitchell, Margaret Atwood are remarkable storytellers; Buber, Tillich, Drucker, Oncken, incredible thinkers.

Susan Daminato provided some initial feedback on how to tell a story and Linda Kenyon, as an editor, has been more than patient as I struggled with verb tense, punctuation, and meaning. Mark Connolly deserves credit for the design work and Marion Woeller for the line renderings. Their work, in combination, has made the book more accessible and enjoyable.

Dave Chilton, Lance Secretan, and Gloria Smith shared without reservation what they know about publishing a book. Their openness has helped immensely.

As collaborators, you gave me all the fun.

Stephen Baetz
St. Jacobs, Ontario
Canada

Introduction

As an undergraduate, I was convinced that universities were in the business of taking the simple and making it complex. I have spent the rest of my life making the complex simple.

So with this book. Its purpose is to take the mystery and complexity out of the change process.

I recognize that with such a claim I may be misunderstood. I am not suggesting that making a change within an organization, team, family, club, or association is easy. Nor would I take the position that change situations don't arrive with layers of ambiguity, conflicting agendas, and varying expectations. They do. But knowing how to make change happen doesn't have to be hard, complex, and painful.

Daily experience and observation have taught all of us some obvious truths about change. The most evident is that successful change-makers are people literate. At a gut level, they recognize that people want to be involved and participate in the decisions that affect them; they encourage others to be responsible, and they care about the people who are involved with the change.

Beyond that, change-makers can define what business they are in and what business they ought to be in.

Only once you have a vision of the future can you pull others forward. As well, they shape strategy from the valley of paradox and they plan to be successful.

All simple notions.

I suppose the more difficult part is knowing just how to do all that.

The challenge I faced was to discover how to communicate the fundamentals of change with clarity and simplicity. Of course, one option was to write yet another text loaded with theoretical constructs and case examples. But the bookshelves are already heavy with these tomes.

The challenge pushed me to think about how I have learned and how I have watched many others learn. Textbooks, I observed, have had less impact than I thought they might. Laundry lists, charts, tables, and graphs cemented by third-person, scientific commentary were soon forgotten or filed under the dreaded heading of "interesting" ... but they didn't act to encourage change.

Stories, fables, parables, and poetry speak to my heart. They teach without telling; they instruct without scolding. Stories nudge. They help to make meaning and sense.

If told well, they never end with a period but always with a question mark. They have caused me to think, to join the journey, and to be part of the learning.

It is for these reasons that I have chosen to communicate with you through a story.

If you are a hard thinker who has been used to third-person, objective descriptions, you may find the story format unsettling as you travel unfamiliar terrain. I do invite you to take the journey, however. As you do, leave behind your rules of what is absolutely logical and orderly. Play for awhile with the improbable and the impossible.

This story invites you to come to Wasiswill, a place where past, present, and future all run together. Here you will be asked to stretch your perspective and get caught in the magic of an attic. Give yourself permission to become part of the dialogue of change.

If you are a soft thinker, you will find the story format an easy read. You will move into the attic and you will never really be sure whether it is place or time. You may not be able to tell whether those in the attic are real and distinct individuals or whether they are the voices of the complexities within the character of The Kid. But because of who you are, you will allow yourself to play with the possibilities. Enjoy.

As with any story, you will bring your own perceptions and experiences. Your view will help you to see to your heart. As you read, you will discover that it is as much a story about personal change as it is a story about organizational change, as much a story about listening as it is about self-management, as much a story about relationships as it is a story about responsibility.

My guess is that when you finish reading, you will have some useful questions and your own personal guide for making organizational change.

Stephen Baetz

To my Wasiswill family,
Marilyn, Matthew, and Joel,
who touch me with the magic of
their insight, vitality, love,
and encouragement

Futures Past 1

THE KID WASN'T CERTAIN whether this was a reward or not. Sure enough his title had changed. He had been told by the President that his contribution, when he was Director of Engineering, had been recognized and valued by the organization. Earlier in his career, this kind of tangible prize would have made him feel the race was worth it.

But today it didn't.

Had the cynicism that he had seen in so many of the senior people finally found a home with him?

Odd how they had been driven by an ambition to gain promotions only to find that their ability to make change didn't increase dramatically just because they had moved into the corner office. That reality had turned so many into the organization's severest critics, hollowed cynics who attempted to pretend that they were not part of the problems they articulated.

Or was it that today he finally recognized that he was leaving his vocation as an engineer. He doubted that this was the problem. The truth was he hadn't done any real engineering in years. When he moved into the management ranks, he had come to grips with the idea that he was now a voyeur, he would only watch others doing the doing.

He did concede, however, that as the new Vice President of Planning, he needed to develop additional skill sets, especially in trend analysis and financial planning. A couple of seminars would put that issue to rest, he thought.

There was no victory in this win. The Kid didn't like it. He liked less not knowing why he felt unsettled.

Emily had called him at the office and told him she had just seen her last patient. She was now off to the hospital to handle some kind of crisis. He had been too preoccupied to hear the details but understood the message: she would be home late, probably around nine. That was fine with him, he told Emily, he had some reading he wanted to do.

He had taken a slightly longer route home, which had given him more time to think. If he remembered correctly his Business 100 text had mapped out a planning model in flow chart format. Such an outline would at least give him a start. He pulled into the drive, gathered the paper, read the disaster headlines, and then headed for the attic.

Cobwebs, dust, and streaked sunlight hung the rafters in gauze. Paper turning yellow melted with leather and mothballs. It smelled yesterday. For The Kid, the past was not time, it was place. This place.

Photographs defined his family and community; ribbons, trophies, and certificates, his accomplishments. Books chronicled his intellectual path, art his emotional journey. Emily's things now mingled with his. The newer stuff was their children's, perhaps soon to leave when university was over for them.

The disorder of it all was a source of amusement for Emily. It was the only place in The Kid's life where chaos was king. He wanted it that way, needed it that way. This was where he had always retreated when the heat was on and he needed a haven of quiet reflection. When play became too rough, demands too great, the attic always soothed and quieted. From here he could plan his next move, wrapped in the comfort of memory.

Nothing was in its place. It was all his place, his time. This was magic.

His books, he thought, were piled near the dormer. He tightroped his way across the attic, balancing between a globe and the boxes of letters Emily had kept from when they were courting, landing in the armless rocker from his grandparents. From here, he saw his world, the record of futures past.

Reaching back, he grabbed the text on top, *Introduction to Psychology*. Psych was reported to be a bird course in the first year. The trouble was that it didn't have the same scientific discipline that his Engineering courses had. Odd how the prof had spent the first week of lectures trying to position it as a science. Only then might it have enough value to be studied.

The third-year books must be in the pile behind. Moving to the edge of the rocker, he stretched for the solid blue he thought was Biz 100. As his hand groped for the wisdom of Drucker, Maslow, and Herzberg, as well as the fundamentals of marketing, spreadsheet analysis, and inventory management, it brushed Abernathy, a basset hound of a few decades past.

Soft, sad eyes spoke no judgement. Abernathy cuddled back when held, had supported The Kid through thunderstorms, had listened when Philip moved. Not fun but always there. Abernathy is comfort.

"It's been some time."

The Kid paused, cocked his head to the door, certain that Emily couldn't be back, and reached again.

"Something troubling you?" Abernathy asked gently, his left eyebrow rising and collecting half his face.

Their eyes met, they connected ... once more.

"How'd you know?"

"Because you're here. Last time was the day before you and Emily were married. Jitters, second guesses, it's pretty normal stuff."

"You're right," The Kid grinned, "I forgot about that."

"And now?"

"And now ... work."

Abernathy knew not to speak unless it improved on silence.

"Today I was promoted."

"To ..."

"Vice President, Planning."

"... and you're not thrilled?"

"I should be."

"... but?"

"I'm not sure what it is. In the past, the Planning job has been seen·as a bit of a plum, an opportunity to gain visibility in all parts of the organization. The department is smaller but the opportunity to influence is bigger than it has ever been."

Abernathy knew to only nod.

"I move from a line to a staff position, reporting to the President."

"So that's how the job is positioned ..." Abernathy shifted slightly, resting his head on his paws.

"The President told me in confidence that he wasn't satisfied with how the function was carried out, merely a short-term, one-year operational planning focus. The mandate now is to be strategic. In his words –" The Kid now lowered his voice an octave in mock imperative "–'I want the planning function to move us boldly into the 21st century.' He wants us to take on a new shape. Interesting rhetoric but I'm not sure what it all means."

"What do your instincts tell you?"

"Nothing, absolutely nothing."

"So that explains the retreat to the books. You're trying to trap new ideas, to find the formula?"

"It's worked in the past. When the going gets tough ..."

"... the tough come to the attic." Abernathy felt that he and The Kid had been through enough together to try that gentle nudge. The Kid didn't, perhaps more accurately couldn't, hear.

"Everybody is to think and behave *strategically* in the future, according to the President. I know how to project plan, have since I was a junior engineer. Gantt charts and critical paths are second nature to me. But 'everybody thinking and behaving strategically' is an agenda I can't get my head around." As he said this, his shoulders slumped, feeling the burden.

Abernathy had both eyes closed now – he listened better with no distractions. The long silence told him that The Kid needed help. "So what's the metaphor?"

The Kid was confused. "What do you mean 'the metaphor?'"

"Language, it seems to me, is more than a string of words to be taken literally. H. Dumpty was right when he sat on a wall and said, 'When I use a word, it means just what I want it to mean.'" Abernathy opened his eyes half way to see if he was being heard. Reassured, he continued. "Words have no absolute meaning, people do." He knew that line would be tough for an engineer so he waited a moment to let it seep in.

"Others often tell us what they really mean between the lines in metaphor and analogy." This time he waited for dramatic effect. "The message is in the metaphor."

Contact was made. "So what I need to do is listen to the President's metaphor to figure out what he really wants?"

A nod.

"Why didn't he just tell me? Who needs to be guessing?"

Abernathy smiled fondly. This was typical of The Kid. Everything was supposed to be straight up, defined, prescribed. Ambiguity, nuance, and subtlety were banished. That was the way order was created. Abernathy lifted his head, half-opened his eyes. "Why do you want the world to be different than it is?"

Shades of Emily. "Point well taken." Sitting back in the rocker, The Kid locked his hands behind his head and searched the rafters with his questions. "What is the President's metaphor, his real message? What might the agenda be?"

Abernathy knew that these were not questions for him to answer. His eyelids dropped. He returned his head to his paws.

"What the President said is that he wants us to move boldly into the 21st century ... he wants everyone to think and act strategically ... words you'd use to describe a game, a chess game. It feels like he is looking for our advantage, something that might give us the edge, more than he is looking for an operational plan that defines who is going to do what over the next 12 months.

"Is the implication that we currently don't know what the issues are in the organization, that we are not moving in a focused way, or that our time horizon is too close to our feet? There could be some credence to that, it fits with other messages ... he's talked about us as dinosaurs, slow to move, with little thought, ravaging only what we see.

"But the interesting thing in the description of the mandate is the word *everybody*. He wants everybody in the organization involved in our future. Do you know what that means?"

The Kid was now leaning forward, looking right at Abernathy who lifted his head, but knew to keep quiet.

"He wants the organization transformed from one that is top down to ... " he stopped in mid-sentence, realizing that he really didn't know what the ending was, "... to something that is ..." he was grabbing now, "... different." As soon as he said it, he knew how insufficient the word was.

The Kid looked for perspective. He began slowly as he attempted to organize his thinking. "The President wants an organization that is changed, can change, can make change. The dinosaur has to die."

That was the closest to metaphor Abernathy had ever heard The Kid get.

"My challenge," The Kid went on enthusiastically, "is to help the organization to change ... and to make change." He paused to let some of the implications settle. "This is more than just a planning job, especially if everyone is to be part of the change-making process. I have a chance to shape the very nature of how we act as an organization."

Abernathy now began to stir, shifting uncomfortably, as if prodded. "Is your organization not doing well?"

"Quite the contrary. All the indicators are positive. We've been described in the media as vital and competent, touted as a low-cost producer." Abernathy could hear the satisfaction in The Kid's voice.

"If it works, why change? Just keep doing what you have always done." It was hard to tell whether Abernathy was playing the devil's advocate or sharing a fear of his own heart.

The Kid was either listening intently or wrapped up in his own thoughts. Either way, silence was the result.

Abernathy scratched his ear, lifted an eyelid then dropped it again. "People can get hurt when change occurs, and once change has started, it's hard to control the speed at which it happens. It's like a snowball headed down a mountain." Abernathy spoke from his heart.

"You could be right. Are we too committed to making change for the sake of making change?" The Kid's exuberance had diminished. He had taken Abernathy's fears as his own. "Change can hurt."

Now neither knew what to say. Each became an island. Abernathy seemed to be able to live with the questions longer. The Kid was far more impatient. Perhaps the difference was time and demands. Feeling the pressure of the President's mandate, The Kid was the first to speak.

"To tell you the truth Hound –" it had been years since Abernathy had heard that name and he loved the memories "– the only thing I am sure about is that it is my job to help make change happen, so that we are future-makers. The issue of why do it, what impact change has or how to help change happen, I don't have a clue about."

He reached past Abernathy and grabbed his old Business text. "But maybe if I continue to read, I'll start to find some answers." The Kid got up to leave, assessing the tightrope walk back.

"It doesn't feel like I've been much help," ventured Abernathy.

"Not to worry, Hound, you've listened."

Wasiswill Wisdom 2

WASISWILL IS A COMMUNITY that runs from the dormer in the west to the cedar chest in the east, north to the spare shingles and south to the antique deacon's bench. Boxes, bags and pails dot the landscape and provide homes.

It is no place and every place at the same time.

In Wasiswill, no one wears a watch, but everyone knows the time. No one rushes to other places just to say they have been there, but everyone grows where they are. No one frets about what they are wearing or how they appear but everyone knows that the Velveteen Rabbit was right – you're more beautiful when your hair has been loved off.

The residents of Wasiswill sing and whistle every day. They read, they talk, and when they are tired, they rest.

Tale and story are things they prize. Their library, near the rocking chair, is packed with the best literature … *Paperbag Princess, Jacob Two-Two and the Hooded Fang, Love You Forever, Jelly Belly, The Dark, Garbage Delight, Those Words, Blackberry Subway Jam, Red is Best, Whoosh I Hear a Sound, Chocolate Moose,* and of course *The Hardy Boys* and *Anne of Green Gables* … all stories of wonder, imagination, relationships, and love.

For the scholarly or the anxious, there is a reference section filled with texts that may be used in universities. This one specializes in Engineering and Medicine with a smattering of Business and Philosophy.

But Wasiswill residents know that imagination is as important as knowledge, that everyone grows to the light.

Just to the left of the rocking chair is the Wasiswill Meeting Place. Those who live in this community recognize the value of independence but they also know the wisdom of coming together.

It was in The Meeting Place that they agreed to the Wasiswill Code. They posted it on the wall as a reminder of what they know and value in relationships. It is, for the most part, a list of statements about interpersonal responsibility, starting points for building mutual trust and respect:

1. *The person who spills the milk, cleans it up.*
2. *The walls we build to keep others out also keep us in.*
3. *What we fear most, we should face first.*
4. *Be care-full.*

The residents recognize that any code is easier to write than live.

It is in The Meeting Place that we find Abernathy, tail wagging.

As he surveys the community, he sees that Spit has just stuck her head out of her home, a square box filled with white tissue paper. It isn't large but it is comfortable. Spit has no tolerance for housekeeping and this suits her just fine, thank-you very much.

Spit is an apple doll with dark brown, wizened features. Her nose almost touches her chin and her eyes are set deep in her head, giving the impression that she can see right through you. Perhaps she can. She is no nonsense and has an acid tongue that can burn to the heart of an issue.

Three boxes down is Hoot who, when she is not out at night, snuggles into a purple bag with a good book. She pulls the gold draw string tightly closed over her head and can be lost for hours. Hoot thinks, watches, observes.

On the opposite side of The Meeting Place, just inside a green football helmet, is Piggy, the bank. He jingles when he walks, a 1932 penny and a 1948 quarter still inside. He is round and pink and is filled with an immense desire to make things happen.

East of Piggy is Chip. He is the newest of all, a remote-controlled robot, a toy of The Kid's oldest child. By design and style, Chip is an engineer. He is perplexed when rational thought processes and logic don't work. Spit wonders if he has a heart.

Chip is attached to a joystick, most would say unfortunately so, since he often waits for others to give him direction. If any within Wasiswill is fascinated by the new, it is Chip. Spit claims that it is only an intellectual fascination and that Chip is more traditional and staid than most.

It is morning and, as is their habit, the residents of Wasiswill are checking in with one another at The Meeting Place. It is a time to share experience and insight, to reconnect. Abernathy is usually last to arrive. This morning, strangely, he is there first ... and eager.

"You'll never guess who I met last night," Abernathy blurted out as soon as everyone had arrived.

"Alice? Dorothy? Anne? Frank and Joe? Jacob? How should we know?" Spit protested.

"Who?" punctuated Hoot.

"The Kid."

"The Kid?" asked Chip. "He is back from university?"

"Not your kid, The Kid. Your kid's the kid of The Kid," Piggy explained to Chip. Strangely, everyone understood.

"Where?" queried Hoot. She loved questions that began with who, what, where, when, how, and why. They always seemed to give her insight into what others thought.

"He was in the rocker last night just before the sun went down. It was like magic to see him again."

"What has he been up to?" asked Hoot.

Abernathy looked puzzled. They really hadn't spent any time talking about what had happened to either of them. They talked about where The Kid was now. "I'm not really sure."

"Whaddaya mean you're not sure?" Piggy was incredulous. "You were talking with him, weren't you?"

"I was but ..."

"... but The Kid's in trouble, I bet, and you spent most of your time listening to his pain." That was Spit. Abernathy nodded. She knew him well.

"So what's the heartburn about this time?" Spit pressed.

Abernathy told the story of the night before and how The Kid was trying to come to grips with how best to make change happen within his organization. As much as he told the content of the dialogue, he shared the feeling and reflected the confusion.

"I do not see a problem. The process for making organizational change is clear and logical," Chip stated.

"Oh is it?" Spit was trying to keep the sarcasm from her voice, but everyone except Chip could hear it.

He continued undeterred. "Making change within an organization is fundamentally a top-down driven planning process. Senior management sets profit and revenue targets for the next year ..."

"Let me guess," Piggy interjected, "Specific objectives follow from goals, plans follow from objectives."

"Exactly. Once you know what your boss' goals and objectives are, you can write your own under that umbrella. Each plan complements the fiscal targets set at the top. The result is a 'no surprises' contract. Every employee knows what is expected of them and every employee knows what every other employee is supposed to be accomplishing."

Spit managed to hold her tongue, but Piggy couldn't. "And the end product is a massive planning document that is filled with detailed description."

"Correct, a document is the result. It just provides everybody with a handy reference."

"And sits unopened on each manager's desk."

Chip was starting to hear the sarcasm and doubt. "No. The plan is to be used actively by managers. As it is being developed, there are sign-off points by managers all along the way. Monitoring points are determined before the fact ..."

"... so everyone can identify deviations to plan and spend endless hours explaining them away and denying any responsibility for outcome." Spit couldn't contain herself any longer. "The unsuspecting get hung while the guilty run for cover."

Chip looked to the others for confirmation of his approach. None was found. "This is just basic management: plan, organize, direct, and control." He was puzzled at the silence of the others. "These are fundamental MBO principles. I am not proposing anything new."

"Exactly." Spit was going for a point.

"Surely the worthiness of an idea," Hoot intervened, "is not proven by how new or old it is."

"Point well made," Spit allowed, "but the fact is, planning is an engineered approach to making change and is out of step with the realities we are facing now. A planning mentality for change-making, with its if/then thought processes, is a waste of energy and effort. Change doesn't happen with a control mind-set ... and that's what MBO is at heart." She folded her arms, certain that she had just offered the last and complete word on the issue.

Piggy was bursting with impatience. "You're right Spit, most planning is a waste of time. Since future shock rarely does, it means that realities are changing so quickly that it is folly to do any planning at all."

"Are you recommending no planning at all?" Hoot questioned.

"Just think about it," Piggy insisted, "you plan on the basis of the variables and realities that you understand today but by the time you get around to putting those plans into action ... say six to nine months in the future ... everything around you has changed. So what you end up doing is implementing yesterday's plan in a tomorrow environment."

No one said a word, so he felt compelled to continue, speaking with dramatic emphasis in an effort to disguise his uncertainty. "Don't teach people how to plan better, teach them how to react."

Chip was unable to respond. This argument ran in the face of all the reading he had done in the Library, although he felt a certain genetic kinship to the notion of quick response time.

Spit glanced at Hoot who was silent and then to

Abernathy who was motionless. She couldn't keep quiet, but at the same time, tried to choose her words care-fully.

"I am amazed, Piggy," she said slowly, "that from what I said, you concluded that we shouldn't plan at all."

Abernathy stirred, "We all know about Piggy's strong bias towards action, you shouldn't be surprised." This was a statement of reality, there was no judgement in Abernathy's voice.

"We see what we believe," Hoot noted.

Piggy felt both an obligation to clarify his position and a desire to pull back from it slightly, fearing that it might be a tad tenuous. "I just think we need to develop a mind-set that helps people to perceive the changes that are happening around them *sooner*. If they can see the present realities more quickly, they can then act in help-ful ways. I just think all this MBA-type analysis is over-rated. We need more people seeing what is there and then doing something about it." Piggy checked to see if his argument had taken.

"Let me see if I understand this." Spit hated para-phrasing, but had realized that all too often she failed to hear others, only to discover later on that she really agreed with them. "You want people who are more per-ceptive to what is around them?"

"Yup."

"So that they have the ability to respond to what they see?"

Piggy nodded his consent.

"You want people who are perceptive and flexible."

"Exactly!"

"Well, so do I." They had found some common ground. "The point that I was trying to make," Spit emphasized, but her voice had softened somewhat, "is that a top-down planning system with goals, objectives, and plans under goals, objectives, and plans is highly control oriented and is no longer a useful change-making strategy."

Abernathy perked up. "You feel planning alone is too narrow an approach to the broader issue of change." There were times like this when everybody thought that Abernathy had vacated only to discover he understood it all, the way it was meant.

An uneasy silence followed, almost like Abernathy had ended the discussion with a period.

"You said Spit," Chip finally ventured, "that top-down planning is an insufficient solution in today's environment. Is the information I have been reading out of date?"

Spit admired Chip's willingness to continue the discussion. She chose not to comment on his reading habits: now was the time for logic. "First of all, top-down planning runs counter to the needs of today's employees. Second, too many planning processes lack vision and leadership, lack soul, passion, feeling. Third –" this was her final point but not necessarily her strongest "– the plans are owned by only the senior few in an organization."

"Secretan, Mintzberg, Moss Kanter and others," Hoot observed, "have made similar, if not complementary, observations on more than ..."

"Come on, Hoot," Spit interrupted, "What I said is nothing more than common sense."

"But you yourself have often said that 'common sense rarely is.'"

"Well," Spit sputtered, "perhaps quoting the pungently insightful is valuable, on occasion." Everyone smiled, even Spit herself.

The sun was now fully above the horizon. Wasiswill

took on a new complexion as the day started to happen.

Hoot picked up a book, yawned, and suggested that they return to The Meeting Place later and explore further some of the observations Spit had made.

After some minor grumblings about how busy everyone was, they agreed to reconvene next weekend.

To Wonder 3

MAGIC IS HARD TO REPRODUCE. Not slight of hand, not deception, real magic. The kind of experience that gets you thinking on a different plane, reminds you that there is still more to experience and learn, makes you quiver in the gut. Magic is not bound by time, it is more connected to place and people.

The trouble most of us have with magic is that we want to use it to escape or get away from something. We want some misery to vanish so we can feel good again. We haven't learned what Dorothy discovered on the Yellow Brick Road – there is no wizard who will deliver you.

But real, honest-to-goodness magic pushes you *towards*. It invites you to take new risks, to see the world in a different way, to wonder.

The attic was a magic place for The Kid. Sure enough, he often went there to escape when the heat was on, but once there, he would allow himself to get on the rollercoaster, to balance on the tightrope, to stand on the edge.

Just ten days after his conversation with Abernathy, he found himself back in the attic again. What fascinated The Kid about his magic place was a strange paradox; it was only in a safe environment like this that he would risk or take a chance on a new idea, feeling, or behaviour. Security allowed him to risk. But then the more he thought, the more it made sense. "If I felt insecure," he concluded, "I would want to hold on even more tightly to what I have."

He rested comfortably with that insight, but only for a moment. If that were the case, he mused, why had it been such a long time since he'd come to the attic? Had he lost his sense of wonder and magic? Had he made a choice to stop growing that he hadn't realized? Was it easier for him to gravitate to the defined and the predictable? He really wasn't sure where these questions would take him, or why he had returned to the attic so soon after his last visit.

What puzzled The Kid most was that Abernathy wasn't where he thought he had been when he left. As he looked around, he had this sense that *everything* wasn't where it had been when he left. How curious, he thought to himself, but maybe his attention to detail wasn't what it used to be. Either that, or ... but that was too preposterous to contemplate ... but it did help explain why he could never find anything in the attic.

The morning sun came streaming in the window and created a drowsy warmth. He thought it as wise to wait for Abernathy as to· search for him ... his mind wandered ... a lazy stroll ... in no direction ... in every direction ... sleep seemed a therapy ... perhaps he was working too hard or was it the frustration that exhausted him ... where was Abernathy ... there were things to do on his Saturday agenda ... he and Emily had squash at two ... never the last shot that does you in, always the second last ... was it exercise or competition ... time doesn't matter ... so what if I'm late ... the clock isn't there to rule you ... magic is not bound by time ... am I dreaming or am I awake ... I know this is the time in between ... time, time, time ... what did Oncken say, "God gave us time so everything didn't happen at once" ... there must be some relationship somewhere between time and event ... do we use a clock because we have lost the ability to tell time by event ... my gawd, there must be an insight there for a planner ... I should get up and write that down right now so I don't forget it ... if it really is good I'll remember it ... Abernathy ... won't I feel foolish if I dreamt us meeting the other night ... I wasn't dreaming all those other times ... was I? ...

"You're back."

... what about my back ... I know I should take more care of it, Emily ... yes, yes lift with the knees ...

"You're back, I said."

The Kid began to realize the voice was not his own but he found it difficult to pull himself towards the voice, to connect. The Kid could sense something thumping at his ankle.

"Challenging was it?"

He knew that voice ... and the thumping wag. Abernathy.

"Challenging yes, and rewarding. The book I took with me the last time gave me a starting point for developing a planning model for our organization. I did a little tinkering with it and it should work."

Abernathy forced a smile, but his eyes told his story. "What did you come up with?"

"The model has the Senior Executive Team – SET I called them – establishing financial targets three years out. At the same time, they present white papers to each other that articulate their understanding of what strategies and tactics need to be deployed to make those targets achievable."

Ouch, Abernathy thought, SET, targets, white papers, articulate, strategies, deployed. Bizbabble. No soul. He pushed himself to act interested. "That's what SET does?"

"In part. SET sets the table for the OPG – Operational Planning Group – each year. Well actually the September prior, they meet for three days in a retreat environment and ..."

The Kid went on and on, mapping out in infinite detail what happened at each level. He defined key responsibilities and accountabilities for both SET and OPG and, as if that weren't enough, he described how the system was top-down with lots of senior management buy-in. He enthused about controls and the attached monitoring system. As he did, Abernathy smiled, nodded, and paraphrased what he heard, but he began to realize the value of a watch, a convenient signal to close down a conversation.

The President, The Kid declared, was very supportive of the draft he had presented. The only glitch was some resistance by the middle management group. The Kid figured they would all fall in line as soon as the senior executives sent out the word that this is the way it is going to be.

Abernathy couldn't even force a smile. His head retired to his paws, but The Kid was oblivious. Neither of them noticed that Chip had arrived and taken up a seat on the edge of a roll of old material.

The Kid was in full flight and mid-sentence, extolling the virtues of checkpoints when deviations would be reviewed and explained, when he caught a glimpse of Chip. The Kid was sure he hadn't been there before. Abernathy heard The Kid's voice drop, looked up, and saw the two eyeing each other oddly.

Ever the gentleman, Abernathy carried out a round

of introductions. The Kid indicated that he thought Chip looked vaguely familiar but couldn't remember if Chip belonged to child number one or two.

Chip asked The Kid to continue but, to Abernathy's chagrin, The Kid started from the top. When the explanation was finally complete, Chip couldn't contain himself. "I was not so far off base after all," he proclaimed, giving a victory wink in Abernathy's direction. "This is a win for system and logic."

Abernathy now refused to speak, not wanting to fuel an old fire. It was at that moment The Kid recognized Abernathy's passive posture. "What's up Hound?" Chip looked surprised, he hadn't heard Abernathy called that before.

The Hound of Wasiswill recounted the dialogue that had happened in The Meeting Place with Spit, Piggy, Hoot, Chip, and himself. After The Kid rekindled memories associated with all the other players, Abernathy shared the conclusions from the dialogue: that planning is an insufficient strategy for making change and that top-down planning in particular is out of touch with the realities of today's employees.

The Kid's first instinct was to argue, to press his own point. But somehow or other he knew that the magic could only happen if he was open. He worked to avoid a defensive position. "What supports those conclusions?" he asked, recognizing that *how* a question is asked speaks as loudly as *what* is asked.

"If you're really interested why don't you join us tomorrow just after the sun goes down. We've arranged to meet then to talk about how the needs of employees have changed," Abernathy suggested.

"You'll all be there?" The Kid asked.

"Just like magic."

Sesame Street Needs 4

THE ATTIC IS A DIFFERENT PLACE at night. Light from the street lamps melds with the moonlight to create a stardust wash. A mirror placed near the window reflects some of the light to the rafters.

In The Meeting Place, as agreed, were Abernathy, Hoot, Piggy, Chip, and Spit. Each had taken their favourite place. Like the day before, Chip was sitting on the roll of old material, Abernathy on the floor between Chip and the rocker. Hoot had perched herself on the end of a bambo fishing pole that was leaning up against a corduroy-covered ottoman. Piggy had ensconced himself in an old woollen sweater that had taken the shape of a wingback by lining a mitre box. And Spit, she refused to sit. Standing and walking kept the circulation going, she claimed. Occasionally, she would lean against an old milk bottle, one that was curved at the top for cream.

Abernathy opened. "Chip and I met The Kid yesterday morning, hard to tell if he had been there all night."

All eyes moved his way as if to say, "And ..."

"And we invited him to join us tonight." A few raised eyebrows resolved themselves into approving smiles when they saw others at ease. "Since we met the last time, The Kid has developed a draft of a planning model that he has presented to his boss," Abernathy continued.

"Let me guess, top-down, highly centralized, with lots of sign-offs and ample controls." Spit knew The Kid well, in fact knew the whole family well over several generations.

Abernathy nodded, either lost for words or disappointed, no one could tell.

"But the boss is positive and enthusiastic about the model," injected Chip, "and so is The Kid."

"Either that or his enthusiasm is a disguise for a real lack of certainty." Abernathy merely made the observation, looking neither one way nor the other.

"'Methinks he doth protest too much' – Shakespeare." That was Hoot giving due credit to the source.

"It really doesn't surprise me." Piggy had now shifted forward and was engaged in the discussion. "Many organizations don't know the difference between operational planning and strategic planning. The Kid's presented an operational planning format and, since they're probably new to planning, they assume that what they have is a strategic plan. I'll bet, Abernathy, the recommendation is to have the planning term be for more than one year."

"Yes, I think he mentioned a three-year rolling period."

"He did," added Chip, "but I do not see ..."

Piggy went on despite Chip. "We've all seen this happen before. An operational planning format is used beyond one year and everyone assumes that they have a strategic plan. The big banks concluded the same thing years ago. But long-range operational plans are not strategic plans."

With that, he got to his feet and went on

mischieviously. "It all assumes, of course, that so much planning will make you light of foot and responsive." He then did a jig he had learned when he was younger, jingling with every step. Stabilizing, he continued, "I believe, as you know, that planning tends to be more of a burden than a help." He flopped back into his seat, exhausted.

Chip was confused. His system was in overload. "Help. Slow down. What is the difference between an operational plan and a strategic plan?"

This was where Hoot excelled. Her reading and observation gave her perspective. "In strategic planning, you determine which key strategies will give you the edge, assuming, of course, that you know what business you're in."

"That should be easy enough," Chip responded.

"It seems so," Hoot continued, "but is a newspaper in the business of putting ink on paper or is it in the business of selling perishable information? Each definition generates altogether different strategies and action plans."

It was Piggy's turn. "Is an education system in the business of teaching students or is it in the business of helping students learn ... and if they can answer that one, the next obvious questions are 'teach what' or 'learn what' and 'who are the students.'"

"Does a software company design and develop software," asked Spit, "or does it sell solutions to manipulate data? Each requires different strategies."

Chip's circuits were beginning to heat up as he tried to keep pace with the examples and think about the implications. He wanted to get in the game himself, but it was moving too fast. Even Abernathy was having fun. "Is a corner store in the business of selling groceries or is it in the business of selling convenience?"

"Does a bank sell financial security," Piggy was dealing with an issue close to his heart, "or does it merely sell investment certificates, high interest accounts, and mortgages?"

"Or is it in the business of producing and selling information?" Hoot added.

Spit was ready with another. "Does a travel company organize and sell vacations or does it sell a dream, an escape?"

Chip thought he understood and was ready to try an example. "Does a restaurant prepare and sell food or a dining experience of some variety or convenience or fun or nutrition?"

"Nutrition?" was the chorus back.

Chip's control panel dimmed. "I was just brainstorming."

"But you've got the idea," Hoot reinforced. "Once an organization comes to grips with the definition of its business, strategies can follow. Take a hotdog stand as an example. Let's say that it resists the easy definition, 'we are in business to sell hotdogs,' and it comes to the conclusion that it is selling convenience to those working in the downtown core. That definition would require it to develop strategies related to efficiency." Hoot recognized there was more to be said but stopped there.

Abernathy suggested it might be an interesting exercise for everyone to write a definition of *what business they were in* and *who their customers were*. The suggestion seemed like a confrontation, so everyone avoided responding.

Spit tried to get things back on track. "A strategic plan has impact in the long term but is not a long-term plan," she pointed out as she jumped out of the way of a large foot that knocked over the bottle she was leaning against.

"Hey! Watch where you're stepping!" Spit muttered a few expletives and composed herself as The Kid settled into the rocker.

"Sorry I'm late," he apologized.

"People with watches always are," Hoot observed.

The Kid grinned. That was Hoot, she had an uncanny way of finding explanation. He reached over and shook Piggy's hand, a formality they had always observed. He and Spit embraced as old friends do. Each had a healthy respect for the other. If it was other than the two of them, it would have been called affection. Chip, Abernathy, and The Kid exchanged nods.

"Have you already started without me?"

"Yes and no," Abernathy responded, "I was telling them about the initial positive response you got from the President and that took us into a discussion about the difference between a strategic plan and an operational plan."

With The Kid's interest piqued, Chip recounted the discussion and the examples. Piggy thought to himself that once the initial thinking was done by somebody else, chip technology was pretty good at repetition.

At the end of the explanation, The Kid wanted to talk about the modifications he should make to his draft, but Hoot intervened, noting that the purpose of the discussion was to define the needs of today's workers. Such a definition, she went on to say, might help them understand what kind of approach to change would be workable.

Abernathy thought it was interesting that Hoot wanted to stick to the agenda. Did she understand that refining a planning system was a futile effort when the real focus should be on change, or was she in a hurry to get out while it was dark?

"The person I see in the workforce today," Piggy initiated, "is a much different person than when I first started." He shifted back in his chair to reminisce. "I started at the bottom. That's where everybody new started. You knew that if you worked hard, made a contribution, it'd be recognized and you'd get the next small step up the ladder. In fact, after about a month on the job you had a real clear idea of what the career path was. You worked through several clerk levels to Lead Hand and from there to Supervisor and ... "

"... Manager to Regional Manager to General Manager to Vice President to Executive Vice President to President." Spit knew the pattern.

"And usually," Piggy continued, "it was within your functional area. No moving like The Kid just did from Engineering to Planning. We kept our nose to the grindstone, did what we were told, and stayed with the same organization from school to retirement. Your relationship with your boss controlled your destiny with the organization."

Now he leaned forward to make his point. "I'm not saying that's the way it should be today, I'm just saying that's the way it was."

Abernathy, Hoot, and The Kid nodded in agreement. The Kid was amazed that this group knew so much about how organizations functioned. They obviously had been out of the attic at times he wasn't aware of.

Spit moved to a scribbler in the corner. She grabbed an old wax crayon and began to speak. As she did, she drew a large mushroom shape on the pad. "The pyramid is out. Today organizations look more like mushrooms than pyramids. Individuals still come in the bottom and work for a while in Production ... but then they begin to look around at jobs in Quality Assurance ... they play there for a while and move over to New Product Development."

As she talked she drew a line that zigzagged across the page. "From New Product Development it might be on to Tech Support. Career paths are no longer straight up, they are more horizontal. There's not the same ambition to make it to the top."

Piggy built on the point. "I was at a seminar the other day and the leader asked a group of 30 how many wanted to become the senior executive of their organization and not one hand went up. She then asked how many people wanted to have career satisfaction and there was a forest of hands. Ask my generation those questions and we all would have said we wanted to be at the top. It was dog eat dog."

Abernathy winced. Piggy apologized for the poor choice of words. He knew how much he resented comments about pulling someone's bacon out of the fire.

Piggy went on. "Shoot, we didn't even know how to spell career satisfaction. In that same seminar, we were asked two other questions. 'How many of you are absolutely convinced that you are going to retire with the organization you are currently with?' I was the only one to put up my hand. And then we were asked, 'How many of you would go work for another organization if you were given greater job scope and challenge?' Everybody there said they would. That would've been unheard of in my day."

"That's exactly the point," Spit emphasized. "Today's workers are more loyal to their careers than to their organizations. Don't misunderstand me, while they are with you they will work hard, contribute, and they won't tell family secrets ... but they rarely see the organization as the only one they will work for."

Abernathy twitched his right ear, almost like putting up a hand as a signal to get in on the dialogue. "Organizations aren't as loyal as they used to be either. There was a time when it was a womb to tomb mentality, you stuck by them and they stuck by you. Now organizations will sell off divisions, close them down, or restructure, if it is to their advantage."

"Maybe it's a bit of the chicken and egg argument. Which came first? A change in the individual's definition of loyalty or a change in the organization's definition," commented Piggy. "Either way, loyalty ain't what it used to be." Abernathy agreed.

Hoot had been out and about more than many of them and she felt compelled to clarify an earlier point. "What's complicating things these days is downsizing at the middle management level so there aren't as many opportunities for promotion. Individuals look for challenge *around* them, not just up."

There was general agreement and then a pause.

"The Sesame Street generation has now arrived in the workplace." The Kid was speaking. "If I got in trouble at school, I got in trouble again at home. Authority and power were associated with position and were automatically given to teachers. Without question, they were always right. I learned not to question authority."

Everyone except Chip exchanged knowing glances. "But I found myself telling my kids 'If you think you're being treated unfairly, speak up.' We've got a generation that's learned to question ... everything and everybody. Personal power is more important than position power."

Seeing the approving nods around the room, The Kid continued. "You'll remember this, Spit." She had moved from the pad of paper to lean on the bell of a trombone. "If I did a poor job in art at school, I was told under no uncertain terms never to make a mess like that again. Now when kids bring junk home from school, parents look at them and say, 'My, I like all the bright colours, tell me about it.' As adults, they come to work with the full expectation that any effort will be valued and praised, no matter what the real quality may be." Again everybody except Chip understood this point.

"It's the same with how they work, too." Piggy was back in the discussion. "Several generations ago it was only individual effort that was expected and valued."

"In fact if you used somebody else's ideas on an assignment it was considered cheating," Abernathy observed.

"But now half the projects that are done in school are team projects where everybody gets the team grade." Piggy sat back again, somewhat exhausted.

"So you see," Spit started to conclude, punctuating her words by tapping the bell of the trombone with her pencil, "today's workers expect to be involved in teams that value their input, and if they don't feel they are being challenged and involved, they will go somewhere else."

"They'll do that," Hoot injected, "because there is little desire to get to the top or, for that matter, much opportunity, because of the leaning out at the middle management level."

"Could I go back to that point for a moment?" It was The Kid who was asking. He had moved his rocker aside and was now sitting cross-legged on the floor, just like he used to. "Even though the opportunities may be more limited than in the past, why is there a lack of desire to make it to the top?"

Abernathy wondered if this question was rooted in

The Kid's own struggle – near the top but not wanting to be – or in the struggle he had seen others involved in. It was always so difficult to understand the motives behind any question. He was about to question more but Piggy had already started to answer. "They work fewer hours a week than their parents did ..."

"And watch the clock more, too," Spit quipped.

"... and they know what it's like to have time available to invest in leisure activities, so it becomes a lifestyle consideration in part, I'm sure. They figure, who needs the extra headaches that come with more senior management positions."

"Either that or they feel that there is enough complexity where they are to keep them challenged." This was really more of a question than a statement from The Kid. It got a few shrugs that admitted such an explanation could be a possibility.

Hoot began to stir. Her feathers ruffled and smoothed. "The reasons may not matter as much as the reality. Today people want to be involved and participating in teams, they are looking for fewer top-down answers, and they want to be valued for the contributions they do make."

The Kid's elbows were resting on his knees, his fists supporting his chin. He was far more relaxed than he had been for a long time. Everyone could see ideas were brewing, so they kept quiet. "What we've been saying supports other changes I've seen. We are sharing information more broadly than we did in the past, we are providing more training and education at all levels, and we are wanting management to take on the role of question-asker rather than answer-giver. All of that is in aid of the needs of today's workers."

The penny was beginning to drop. "And that is

why," he continued, "a top-down planning process with lots of sign-offs and controls is going to have very little impact in making change happen in my organization. No wonder the middle managers resisted, they were being dealt out. Senior management may have liked it because they saw they had all the control."

Abernathy smiled. "It seems," he ventured, "that organizations need less management and more leadership as they think about making change and moving into the 21st century."

That sounded right to The Kid but he didn't know what it meant, exactly. He was about to pursue it when Hoot reminded everybody that the stars were bright and they could come back to that issue another day.

The Kid suggested the next evening, but Spit objected, "We've got lives too, you know." You always knew where Spit was, there was never any guessing. So much easier to deal with the Spits of this world than with those who are vague and obtuse, The Kid thought. He even took it a step further. Individuals who can be explicit about their needs increase the chances their needs will be met.

The group did hear that The Kid felt an urgency to make changes to his model and agreed to meet Tuesday at dusk.

Hoot ruffled her feathers again and, before The Kid could notice, was gone.

Inside Out 5

CHIP FOUND HE COULDN'T SLEEP that night. The discussion in The Meeting Place had started to generate a lot of introspection about who he was, what business he was in, and his relationships with others. Instead of spending the night tossing and turning, he returned to his old material to wait.

Just as the first light of morning was beginning to flicker in the night sky, Hoot reappeared on her perch. She was about to fly from there to her purple bag, when she saw Chip waiting. "You're up early. Busy day ahead of you?"

"I never went to sleep."

Hoot realized that such an incomplete explanation was nothing more than an invitation for further inquiry. "What's up?"

Chip, although he had never said so, was completely impressed with Hoot. She was not only logical and thorough – something he himself was programmed to be – she was perceptive. Perhaps, he thought, she was a prototype for the next generation. "It is personal." He hoped this wouldn't scare her away, but then owls don't scare easily.

"Personal, you say," Hoot thought she was sounding more and more like Abernathy, mirroring back what was said.

"It started last night when Abernathy suggested we might want to write a personal statement of what business we were in. Some of us felt uncomfortable with it, so we passed on to something else. Talking about corporate issues is much easier than talking personally."

Not bad at all, Hoot thought to herself. He has some ability for self-evaluation; debugging is probably what he would call it.

"And then I began to realize that I did not understand the needs of today's workers. That caused me to begin wondering what else I did not understand."

Hoot remained expressionless, a page on which to write.

Chip hesitated then sputtered, "I am having problems with my partner." If it was possible for Chip to blush, he would have. "You know that one of Abernathy's daughters and I are now staying in the same box, over by the green helmet. In many ways she was just like Abernathy."

"You said 'was.'"

"Yes, when we began our association, I was attracted by her warmth. She listened and supported and encouraged. I fell in love with her big, brown eyes. She had everything I did not have and needed."

"We are often attracted by what we don't have only to discover it's hard to live with what we don't have," Hoot observed.

Chip detected some double meaning but he didn't quite get it. Oh how he wished he could multi-task! He regained focus and continued. "But in the last little while, she has changed. I am not living with the same individual. She is demanding, she always has to have her own way, she argues with everything I say, criticizes my ideas, and tells me I do not listen to her. She claims that I am insensitive and that I am emotionally aloof. Did you hear that? That I am aloof. I cannot even talk to her like I used to."

"That's quite a list," Hoot reflected.

"Just yesterday she posted a list of duties that I am supposed to perform every day. She says she is tired of having to do it all. And then she says she wants to spend more time together. I am not sure I really want to, to be quite honest."

"That's always a good way to be."

"What? Oh yes." Chip identified this as Hoot's brand of humour ... or was it a message? He got tired of trying to decode all the output that came his way.

Despite not understanding, he went on. "I am living with a stranger. She has changed all the rules. She is making me feel miserable. What is wrong with her?" With that, his power light faded a bit, he was out of energy.

Hoot waited a moment until Chip powered on again. "Did you hear yourself?"

"Yes. How could I not?"

"So many have trouble hearing their own voice."

Chip's screen went blank.

Hoot tried again, "Listen to what you just said to me." She was trying hard to be reflective and not judgemental. "*She* has changed, *she* is demanding, *she* argues, *she is making me feel miserable.*"

"Well *she* is!" protested Chip angrily.

Hoot knew that a fire only burns if it has fuel. Silence was best now. Eventually Hoot tried a gentle confrontation. "*SHE* is?"

"Well is she not?"

"Why do you want to see it that way?"

"See what, what way?"

"That she is the one who has control over how you feel."

"Are you suggesting," Chip started, "that she does not control how I feel?"

Hoot was now aware that for Chip this was a revolutionary idea. To get more familiar with the idea would take time. "Eleanor Roosevelt once said, 'Nobody can insult me without my permission.'" This was vintage Hoot. "That doesn't mean that somebody has to put up their hand and ask if they can deliver a zinger. No, she was saying, 'I'm the one who controls how I feel.' We can't always choose what happens to us but we have all the choice we want in how we respond, how we feel."

"So I cannot blame somebody else?" Chip was testing, tentatively.

Hoot smiled a wise smile, gave think time and then flew from her perch to the pad that Spit had used the night before. She flipped to a clean page and began. "Think of the growth to personal maturity as four steps." As she drew four steps she added the aside, "This is a model that I learned a long time ago and it has helped me put my own growth in perspective."

Chip was listening, he knew he had a lot at stake.

"The first step is denying the facts. This is where individuals don't want to see what is in front of them, they have eyes but they can't see. 'You think I drink too much, no way. I'm European and we learned to drink at home ... I know how to handle it.' There comes a point when they can no longer deny the facts and they move up to the second step, blaming others. They look for somebody else to take responsibility for what is happening or what they are experiencing. 'Sure I may be drinking too much, but my boss is such an ogre.'"

Chip winced, something that Hoot hadn't seen him do before. "That is where I am when I say '*She has changed, she makes me feel.*'"

Hoot knew Chip understood. "At this step," Hoot observed, "we give over personal responsibility for how we feel and act to somebody else."

"And then?"

"Step three, accepting responsibility. This is when the individual owns the milk that they've spilt."

"Now some of the Wasiswill Code is making sense!" Chip exclaimed. "When you really accept responsibility, you do not expect somebody else to clean it up for you. The last step?"

"Problem solving. The individual who owns the problem gets on with doing something about it. Not theoretical planning, but action, doing something about it, the kind of stuff Piggy is always pushing for." Again, Hoot gave time for the idea to register. "The trouble is," Hoot observed as she put down the crayon and flew to her perch, "when it comes to personal responsibility, some people are afraid of heights."

"Like me," Chip acknowledged with some degree of resignation.

Abernathy would keep quiet, Hoot thought to herself, so she did.

"I have been outer directed too long," Chip concluded, "I have given control of my joystick to somebody else." Hoot wasn't sure but she thought she saw a small tear of regret trickle down Chip's face. "*She* is not the problem. If I learned to live with myself, I could probably live more comfortably with somebody else."

"Perhaps, Chip."

"But I have been built this way, I am a victim of my designer."

"How you play your cards is more important than what cards you have."

The sun was now a red ball above the horizon. Hoot

wanted to catch forty winks but Chip was just beginning to puzzle some things together. "One of the reasons I may be attracted to a centralized, top-down, control-oriented organization is that it always leaves me someone else to blame if failure occurs."

Now it was Hoot who wasn't understanding, one eye opened curiously wide.

"Yes. I can always say, 'Do not blame me, it was the people upstairs who did not know what they were doing.' I end up avoiding responsibility. In my argument the other day for a top-down planning organization I was just pushing to have my world the way it always has been. You see," it seemed like a funny expression to use when talking to an owl, "participative and involving work-places require that everybody owns the outcome."

"You may very well be right," mused Hoot. "We often seek structures and organizations that reinforce our individual needs."

It was at this point that Chip began to think in a way that was very different for him; he began to think about the psychological dynamics that may exist in an organi-zation. He told Hoot that he had heard many individuals talk about involvement and participation in decision-making, but many of them were clearly unwilling to accept the consequences.

"Accept the consequences?" queried Hoot.

Chip tried to recall what other input he had re-ceived. "Sometimes the price you have to pay is surren-dering your right to grouse." As soon as he used that term, he wished he could take it back. "Sometimes you pay by giving more time and sweat. Sometimes you pay the price by bringing your whole self to work. Sometimes ... "

"Bringing your whole self to work?"

"Yes. Many people just bring their skills to work.

They check them in at 8:30 and out at 5:00." Chip was starting to sound different, almost poetic. "But they refuse to think, take initiative, or dig into their jobs with passion. They bring their hands to work but not their heads or their hearts. There are others who bring their heads but not their hands or hearts. They think but they do not do. They drive Piggy crazy. They do not bring their whole selves to work."

"And you're saying," Hoot clarified, "that if they want involvement and participation, they have to pay the price and bring their whole selves to work?"

"Exactly."

"Spit has an expression, 'You can't blow and suck at the same time.'" Hoot pointed out. "So you can't ask for participation and involvement if you're not willing to pay the price."

"Do you realize the implication of all this, Hoot? Organizations need leaders who are *people literate*, leaders who can help individuals own the full responsibilities that come with increased participation and involvement."

Hoot feared that, with this last line, enthusiasm had turned itself to rhetoric and that anyone who came in contact with Chip today would be saved. She did agree with the point, however. Organizations needed leaders who could read and respond to the needs of others, leaders who could deal with the so-called softer issues.

Wasiswill was now beginning to stir. Hoot was tired and wanted to hit the sack. She double-checked to see if the concern Chip had started with was in perspective. He assured her that it was, that the problem was not "*she.*" It was time for him to start to internalize his joystick.

Personal Business 6

"You will never guess what I have been working on," Chip blurted out as soon as he arrived.

Everyone was in the attic, on time, as agreed. Each had taken the same position as the previous meeting, all creatures of habit. The Kid, sitting cross-legged on the floor, asked, "What?"

"I have been formulating a statement of what business I am in as an individual."

"And ..." Abernathy prompted.

"And it ain't easy." A few knowing glances were exchanged, a few eyebrows raised at Chip's choice of words. "It is just my first draft and I am not sure if it makes any sense to anybody but me."

"Are you saying you're not going to tell us or are you asking us to beg?" To be anticipated, that was Spit.

"I will tell you if you promise to see it as a first draft." They all agreed. Chip now knew the words by heart. "I am in the business of taking personal responsibility for everything that I undertake so that those around me might do the same." He rushed the last part because when he said it out loud he thought it was corny. He waited for the laughter, but none came.

"I'm impressed." Abernathy was always supportive.

Chip needed to provide further clarification, even though none was asked for. "Although that statement is very important to me right now, I realize that I should re-evaluate it periodically." He then shared the insight that he and Hoot had come to the previous night and concluded with the observation, "You know, it is really tough to own your own joystick."

Piggy was wiggling somewhat uncomfortably in his chair. "I, too, tried a draft," he said trying to appear casual about it. Everyone wore a pleased smile. "I made copies that I'll pass around if you're interested."

"C'mon Piggy we're past begging." Spit again. Piggy circulated the draft, and there was a silence as everyone read.

> *I, Piggy B., am in the business of making a positive and worthwhile contribution in whatever I do. My aim is always to be better.*

"I know it's short," he offered, in a mild defense, "but they are supposed to be that way ... aren't they?" It was odd to see Piggy so unsure. The Kid indicated he liked brevity.

Spit couldn't resist. She had to see if he was working at always doing better. "If you had a chance to do it over again, what would you change?"

Piggy was already trying to live what he wrote. "I think I would say, 'positive, worthwhile and *valued* contribution.'" Spit was impressed.

Before long, each individual had taken out their draft and shared it. Abernathy was smiling ear to ear. His suggestion had been heard, and even better, acted on – always a high form of praise.

The Kid noted that he was impressed by how each individual's statement built on their strengths. "Too often we fret about shoring up our weaknesses."

"It's *The Way of the Tiger*," Hoot whispered to Spit.

"Nothing more than common sense, I'd say," countered Spit, "to sell what you've got rather than what you don't have."

"But common sense rarely is."

"Agreed." Spit was pleased that someone had heard what she had said in the past.

With each of them sharing, a spirit of generosity filled The Meeting Place. Some thought of it as trust, others respect. Abernathy knew that it felt good, but no one spent much time talking about it. More importantly, they connected.

"I wonder," Chip thought out loud, "why it has taken me so long to realize that you cannot manage an interpersonal relationship with somebody else until you learn how to manage yourself."

"There are many in the organization that I work in," The Kid observed, "who don't have that insight, and they're a lot closer to retirement than you are. If the truth be known, most of our management development and education does not concentrate on self-management at all. Somehow or other we're expected just to know that stuff."

Unwittingly, The Kid had touched an issue that was close to the heart of both Hoot and Spit. Because they had been around longer, and had seen more, they had become skeptical about much of management education.

Hoot was the first to build on what The Kid had said. "The starting point for management education has to be that common sense principle," with this she winked at Spit, "'treat others as you would like to be treated yourself.' If that becomes your organizing principle, you're on the right track. Second, we've got to start developing the whole person." This point was lighting up Chip's board. "Just teaching skills is insufficient ... we need to shape attitudes that support the skills and provide people with a secure knowledge base so they know *why* they are doing what they are doing. That's the only way to get anybody to act independently."

Chip's control panel flickered and dimmed. Hoot recognized she wasn't as clear as she could be. "We only develop independent individuals when they know how to think."

"Attitudes, skills and knowledge," Chip was repeating to himself, hoping he had captured the input.

Piggy knew about this issue, too. "So much of our education within organizations has just focused on one of those three. If you just teach skills but don't provide the supporting knowledge and attitudes, you end up with an individual who is all technique but can't tell you why they are doing what they are doing. They feel plastic." As soon as that was out of his mouth, he recognized he hadn't been care-full. He turned to Chip and apologized.

Chip said he understood what Piggy was trying to say. Piggy then went on to conclude, "All technique and no substance, who needs it?"

"Those techniques are used to manipulate others artificially," Spit carried on. "Listen to the advice you get on those programs ... praise before you criticize. That's like a game of set 'em up and knock 'em down. Is it any wonder individuals treated that way get cynical about praise? They wait to hear the criticism that they are sure is going to follow. I know the praise isn't even heard. Or another one that gets to me," Spit was on a roll, "is to use money as a carrot to motivate ... sheer and utter nonsense. It assumes we only work for money."

"Or what about the educational process that only

gives you knowledge and ignores any attention to attitudes and skill!" The Kid continued, pointing out how these individuals come with all the theory but not a clue about what to do with it or even how they feel about it.

Now Abernathy's turn. "Or education that focuses on attitude and feeling alone but never teaches skills or provides the learner with the supporting knowledges. We've all seen the fallout from encounter groups."

"Education within organizations should deal with the whole person. That's what you've been saying Chip." Chip felt pleased to have his point recognized by The Kid.

There was a lull in the dialogue as each individual thought about some of the conclusions: real leadership starts with self-management, treat others as you would like to be treated yourself, and management education needs to be approached holistically.

"If we were to develop a set of principles for interpersonal behaviour, what would they be?" The Kid's mind clearly had wandered away from what they had been talking about, but it didn't matter. They had all the time they wanted.

Abernathy got an odd look on his face, almost as if he wasn't sure whether he should say anything or not. He opened his mouth as if to speak, then bit his lip. Spit caught his eye. "Well, Hound, what's cookin'?"

"I don't know if I am speaking out of turn or not, Hoot," he was looking at her, "but I know you've done some thinking about that very topic."

Hoot shifted on the pole, gave a little nod, admitting that she had.

"Well ... " Piggy pushed.

"I should tell you that some of these ideas are not mine ... that is, I didn't make them up. They probably came from all kinds of sources that I'm unaware of." Hoot wanted to give credit where credit was due. "You put them all together and they're me. I call them observations. Principles seems a little pretentious to me." No one understood where the last explanation came from. It was neither suggested nor asked for.

Everyone was silent as Hoot recited her observations slowly.

1. *What you give is what you get.*
2. *Help yourself.*
3. *The best way to change somebody else is to change yourself.*
4. *There are never mistakes, only lessons.*
5. *Things will stay the same unless they change.*
6. *You can't help a person who doesn't have a problem.*
7. *Anything that has been changed, can be changed.*

The best response she could have hoped for, she got: silence.

They were thinking. Quiet could be heard.

Abernathy moved from his usual position with his chin on his paws to a crouch. "All of them complement the Code of Wasiswill," he began, "and so many of them speak to the issue we were just talking about, self-management. That first one, in particular, is bang on." His tail was wagging with excitement. "You give anger, you get anger. You give criticism, you get criticism. Others can only give you what they get."

"But it can work the other way too. You give kindness, you get kindness. You support, others support." As Chip said this, he exchanged knowing glances with Abernathy. "Of course, that first observation relates to the third one, the best way to change somebody else is to change yourself. If I start to relate differently to others, they will relate differently to me." Chip began to wonder whether Hoot had created these observations just for him, but then he concluded that they were more general than his situation.

"I like the simple wisdom of 'Help yourself,'" Spit asserted. "That's been a tough lesson for me ... and as I look around ... it's a toughie for others too. The statement just tells you the truth. You're the one who is on the hook, nobody else is going to save you or rescue you from how you feel, your anxieties, problems, whatever. The problem is," she was now speaking slowly for added emphasis, "for every individual in this world who chooses to play victim, there is somebody who feels the divine urge to rescue them."

"... and that only perpetuates the problem rather than solves it ... 'cause as Hoot said, 'Things will stay the same, unless they change,'" added The Kid.

Piggy's face was scrunched into a knot. The Kid figured that he hadn't understood what was just said so he provided an example from his own experience. "A couple of years ago, when I was a middle manager, I had a person working for me who would willingly take on a project and commit to a deadline. Sure as day follows night, she would encounter a mess of problems, throw up her hands in despair, and tell me that the project couldn't be delivered to deadline. She went into incredible detail about how she was a victim of circumstance and, with that, she became passive and wouldn't help herself."

The group was quiet, fascinated.

The Kid continued. "Being inexperienced, I ran in as her rescuer and saved the day. Of course, what happened time and time again thereafter? The same pattern ... 'yes' to the challenge ... a refusal to help herself when a problem was faced ... and me to the rescue. Things stayed that way, until I chose to change and, as a result, broke the pattern. When I think about it now – dumb, dumb, dumb!"

"There are never mistakes, only lessons," Abernathy reminded.

"All of Hoot's Observations are woven together," The Kid went on. "One of the things that I have to remind myself of daily ... is that you can't help a person who doesn't have a problem. By rescuing that individual and taking the problem away from her, I didn't help her, she didn't become more independent, more capable, more competent. She became more dependent, dependent on me. I got a result opposite to what I wanted."

"If you're not part of the solution, you're part of the problem – Harvey Cox," Hoot validated.

"That is just another reason," Chip pointed out, "why self-management and self-reflection are so important. When leading, you have to understand what your own role is. Self-awareness is the first step towards self-control."

"Not bad, Chip, 'Self-awareness is the first step towards self-control.' I'll have to add that to my collection." Hoot was pleased.

"But it is so true. Until The Kid steps back to look and becomes aware, he does not know he is part of the problem – none of us do."

"I suppose the real good news," Abernathy mused, "is the last item on Hoot's list: 'Anything that has been changed, can be changed.' There's real hope in that observation. It suggests that everything is changeable." He ambled a couple of paces to his right and laid down again. "At the same time, the statement doesn't give you any room to hide."

Chip wasn't following. "Room to hide?"

"You can't hide behind the statements 'That's just the way I am' or 'That's just the way I feel' with the implication tailing along behind that you can't change."

"Gotcha." Everyone grinned at Chip's use of one of Piggy's favourite expressions. "Everything can be changed."

Hoot loved the discussion. Each comment seemed to build on another. As far as Hoot was concerned, The Meeting Place was about being connected as well as about thinking and reflecting.

For Hoot, thought was play. Logic was hide 'n seek. Identifying implications was somersaults in the grass. Brainstorming was kick-the-can. Solution finding was dressing up. Evaluating was hopscotch. Some of the games were played for the sheer joy of it, others for the exercise, still others because there was a real win that could be found.

Hoot was having fun now. Seven simple observations had made all this play. Incredible.

"Remember when you were in grade five," Spit was speaking to The Kid. "You had the messiest room I ever saw."

"What we become is not necessarily what we were?" Chip both added and asked.

"Your mother would ask you to clean it up, you said you would, you would get busy doing something else and never get around to it. But with the pressure of company coming, your mother would whisk into your room and clean it up. It didn't take you long to learn that you would never have to clean up your room."

"You're right, Spit. I played the victim, Mom was the rescuer and things have stayed the same with Mom because *I* never changed the pattern with her." The sheepish grin on The Kid's face turned pensive. "I learned the pattern well from her. When I managed somebody else, I became the parent rescuer to my victim employee. It's alarming to think we take on the role of parent when we become managers."

"Many managers think their job *is* to be a parent," Abernathy agreed. "They define the don'ts, they dole out praise, they coach and correct."

"Does it also follow then that many employees become helpless children, when they relate to their boss?" Chip asked. Then he indicated he really wasn't looking for an answer. "Mature relationships can be hard to find," he concluded.

Work, family, and business examples continued to be used to understand and test Hoot's Seven Observations of Interpersonal Behaviour. It was Abernathy who finally noticed that Piggy had withdrawn from the discussion, his face still knotted. "At the risk of becoming your rescuer and not allowing you to speak up for yourself, what's up?"

"Nothing really." With those words, he recognized he may have given a double message. His face communicated the most. "Don't misunderstand me, I'm in full agreement with Hoot's Seven Observations. I guess I was just thinking ... leadership has got to be more than just the ability to be people literate, to manage yourself, and to live out the Seven Observations, doesn't it?" Piggy had question marks written all across his face.

Spit was quickly back into the discussion. "You're right, it does. Leadership that is going to be viable has to see where it is going, has to have a clear vision."

The discussion returned to how to get organizations to make change and head in the direction of a corporate vision when ...

"You up there honey?" All eyes went to The Kid. It

was Emily. "Hon, you there?"

"Yes, yes I'm here."

"Your boss is on the phone and he wants to talk with you."

"Tell him I'll be right there."

The magic was put on hold.

Insight Out 7

W<small>ITH THE MEETING OVER</small>, Chip made a hasty retreat, explaining that he had a program to rewrite. Spit said she was tired, evidently she wasn't used to late nights. The grapevine in Wasiswill had her seeing an old wooden soldier, a perfect, gentle man who was stunning in his red tunic. Hoot, still grinning ear to ear, flew off for the evening.

Only Piggy and Abernathy were left.

In terms of style and approach, they are different.

Piggy pushes for action and is eager to get on with things. He values a pragmatic solution that can be implemented today far more than a theoretically-perfect one that may never get off the drawing board.

Abernathy is sensitive, caring, and empathic. He always considers solutions that respect the needs of others to be the best. Seeing others grow is his greatest joy. A sensitivity encourages his perception. He can see to the heart.

It is because they are so different that they like one another. They recognize that no one grows with only an image of themselves.

As they headed out of The Meeting Place, they talked about what books they had read lately. Abernathy spoke with care and affection about one of his all-time favourites, *Love You Forever*, Piggy about *Alligator Pie*. Although quite different, these are stories with heart. They talked about movies and theatre, about relationships and accomplishments.

The air was warm, the stars were bright. Piggy and Abernathy talked because they were full. The events of the last week had provided excitement and vitality in Wasiswill. They shared what they had learned.

Abernathy asked Piggy to join him for milk and cookies. The invitation was gladly accepted.

With two huge glasses of milk and a plate of homemade oatmeal cookies, they both settled into large gold pillows, which The Kid and Emily had in their apartment when they were in university.

"You know, Hound," Piggy said taking a long slurp of milk, manners don't really matter when you are with friends, "we sometimes get the impression that it's all within our grasp, that we can control anything we wish if we just put our minds to it."

"It's either that or we think we have no control. One extreme or the other."

"The wisdom, of course, is to know what you can change and what you can't."

Abernathy agreed. "Speaking personally, I know that the only person I can change is myself. That's much the same point that Hoot made in her Observations."

"And if an organization doesn't want to change, it won't."

They sat to hear what they had just said and sipped some more.

"I guess it's back to that old notion," continued Abernathy, "that all you can do is create an environment where others want to decide for themselves to make the change." This wasn't a new or revolutionary idea, by any stretch of the imagination, but they still enjoyed it together. They toasted Wasiswill.

"Dear Hound." Gawd, how Abernathy liked it when friends used that nickname, it proved he was well loved. "Another thought about change."

"Go ahead, Piggy, I'm all ears."

"We don't fear change as much as we fear the unknown." He paused for a moment. "Who said that?" They both shrugged and then giggled, like they had just shared a secret.

"Which means," Abernathy continued after he regained his composure, "that change will be resisted by any individual or by an organization, if there is no vision of what the future might be like."

"Change-makers must be visionaries." Piggy wasn't sure what he meant by that. Did they imagine new futures or did they merely see where the present was headed? In the wee hours of the morning, this was a tough issue to unravel, especially in Wasiswill where pastpresentfuture were always connected, so he let the idea drift.

They toasted The Meeting Place, the exchange of ideas, and friends ... and then they passed the cookies.

They both were grinning silly grins.

"Piggy, a random thought." Abernathy leaned over close to Piggy and whispered, "What gets you to where you are, will often keep you from where you are going."

"Zowie, Hound. What insight!" Piggy added to what he thought Abernathy meant. "There is an incredible temptation for all of us to hold on to what we have and what we know, but if we continue to do that, we will never make the necessary changes a new environment brings us."

"I know that is true of individuals. Do you think it is also true of organizations?" Abernathy walked to the fridge to get another jug of the cold white stuff, refilled Piggy's glass and then his own.

"In spades. I'm convinced that the biggest curse for organizations is success. It blinds them from searching for the new. They have this notion that what will happen to them in the future is what is happening to them now. They lose their edge. Instead of doing something innovative, they try old solutions in a new environment."

They talked and played into the night, one idea fed another, some were connected, some weren't. The longer they talked, the more fanciful they became, the milk and cookies obviously going to their heads.

"Why don't we try a Hoot?" Piggy proposed.

"A Hoot?"

"Yeah, why don't we write down our insights about change, put them up on a poster?"

Abernathy scurried to find a large sheet of paper and a black crayon. They poured more milk and put their heads together. At the top of the page in large bold letters Piggy wrote, Change Insights. When they were done, they had written six words.

Change Insights
1. Change is.
2. Gotta wanna.
3. Inside out.

And then, for whatever reason, Piggy picked up the crayon and wrote a postscript.

P.S. The colour of change is grey.

They both looked at one another, nodded, and agreed it was the right thing to say.

Piggy suggested that he pin up the poster on the wall of The Meeting Place on his way home. At the door, Abernathy turned to Piggy and said, "In the cold light of day, do you think this will make as much sense?"

"I don't know, Hound, but let's post it anyway."

Reading Between the Lines 8

IT IS A HAZY DAWN, AN EARLY MORNING fog has not yet given way to the bright sun. There are no shadows or definition. Everything is round and soft.

As usual, the group was beginning to gather in The Meeting Place to touch base. Spit, Chip, and Abernathy arrived first.

Chip indicated that his reprogramming was progressing. However, when he got into the code to make the changes, he discovered that it was more complicated than he first expected. Spit uncharacteristically commented that she had had a good night. It was always hard to tell whether Abernathy's eyes were half open or half closed; this morning they were definitely half closed.

Spit was the first to notice the poster tacked on the side of a button crate, an antique from Spadina Avenue that Emily had bought when she was an intern. "Was this up here yesterday?" Spit questioned.

"Not that I remember," Chip answered. Abernathy gave a noncommital shrug.

They gathered round. "It's in Piggy's handwriting," Spit blurted. "Big bold letters with those funny curly tails that cross the t's."

"It certainly is brief," Chip commented. "The Kid

would like that."

"Only if it means something," countered Spit. "That old porker is starting to become introspective on us." Spit was grinning.

Porker, Abernathy thought, he's loved too.

Spit tapped her finger on the poster. "And I think it does."

"Does what, Spit?" asked Chip.

"Mean something," Spit retorted. "These Change Insights mean something."

"Change is?" Chip turned to Spit with a you've-got-to-be-kidding look on his face. "How does that make sense?"

"The typical assumption is that the status quo is the normal state and that change is unusual. As a result, change has got a bad name. But just for a moment, make the opposite assumption. Change is normal and to resist change is unnatural." Spit was playing a new kind of hide 'n seek. "Could such a seemingly odd assumption be supported?"

Abernathy was quiet, Chip was having fun watching Spit act like Hoot.

"I think there is support," Spit went on. "Use a biological model to help you think. There is no doubt that nature works to establish a steady state, to maintain a balance. At the same time, it has a tremendous capacity to adapt to the new. What is redundant is sloughed off, the new is accommodated. If this weren't the case, we still wouldn't be standing erect." Abernathy couldn't help but smile. "Nature stabilizes, adapts, stabilizes, adapts – but it is always changing."

"I suppose," Chip was struggling to internalize the idea, "that growth is the metaphor of nature. Sometimes the growth is painful as a natural selection process culls out the weak or redundant. Sometimes the new doesn't survive. Sometimes it is fragile. But, growth is the metaphor, and by implication, that means change."

"If we take that assumption to a logical conclusion, the process of resisting change is unnatural and must be energy depleting." Spit was now doing a somersault. "It isn't too much of a leap of logic then to suggest that resisting change and growth makes us tired, uneasy."

"Some people even claim that it can lead to dis-ease," Chip attempted to take it a step further.

"From my vantage point, Piggy was right on," Spit concluded, "Change is."

Chip pointed to the second insight. "Now that is one I think I understand. Nothing will change unless there is a real willingness. You gotta wanna or you are not gonna." A half-smile came to his face as he played with the new language. "Building on the biological model for a moment, nature will not make an adaptation unless there is a reason for change. Individuals will not change unless they can see some payoff, benefit, or need."

"Oh, oh, this sounds like that old tried 'n true piece of wisdom, there has got to be a WIFM," Spit challenged.

"WIFM?" asked Chip.

"What's in it for me," Spit spelled out. "The explanation usually given is that nobody does anything unless they can see some payoff for themselves."

"You sound less than convinced."

"I am. We do some things for selfish interests because there is a personal WIFM. But personal self-interest alone is too narrow an explanation. We do some things because we believe the group will benefit."

"A WIFU?" Chip suggested. He was a quick study. "What's in it for us."

"Sure. Group, team, or corporate welfare is a significant motivator to action ... maybe even as significant as personal self-interest. Most of us are social by nature. Probably both a WIFM and a WIFU have to be there if change is going to occur."

"So that is gotta wanna." Chip paused to reformat. "Do you suppose that inside out relates back to self-management?" And before anyone could respond, he went on to answer his own question. "The place to start any change process is at the centre."

"Now even you are sounding metaphoric," Spit chided good-naturedly. "But you're right. We talked about self-management for individuals but it is equally true for organizations. There is a strong temptation for organizations to want to change everything but themselves. Sometimes it's government, sometimes unions, sometimes regulatory bodies, the media, or competition. The useful place for them to concentrate their energy is within themselves. They should look at the core, to purpose, traditions, values, strategies, priorities."

Everyone nodded, it made good sense. The Kid would know more about that issue, it might be wise to ask him. "But does anyone have a clue what the postscript is all about?" Chip asked.

"No, and Piggy might not know either. 'The colour of change is grey' looks like an afterthought," Spit concluded.

Abernathy merely shrugged. Spit claimed that Piggy was probably just being playful, that it was like asking what sex is the letter P or how wide is imagination, or how loud is hard.

"Change cannot be a colour. It is not logical. It does not make sense." As soon as Chip had said that he recognized that it was his old program talking. "But then," he went on, "everything does not have to be logical and always make sense." Nice recovery, he thought.

"Piggy should be here soon. The sun is fully over the horizon." The words were barely out of Spit's mouth when Hoot swished in over their heads and landed just by the rocker.

"The Kid is on his way up." Hoot gasped for air to continue. "Apparently he was up late last night after a meeting with his boss. He looks beat or should I say beaten."

With this news, they all scattered, looking for Piggy and agreeing to come back as soon as they found him.

Strategy from Paradox 9

PIGGY IS FOUND, HE HAS SLEPT in after a tough night, he explains. He dresses quickly and they all head back to The Meeting Place.

The Kid is already there, wondering where everybody is and if the magic has failed. He looks like he has been pulled through a knot-hole.

"What's happened?" Abernathy asked gently, as everybody took their usual position.

"The phone call last night was from my boss. He tried to catch me before I left work for the day but we just didn't cross paths. Evidently, there is some resistance forming to my draft of the planning process. Interestingly enough, that resistance is coming from my peers, the Vice Presidents."

"They're now getting pressure from below them," Spit anticipated.

"It appears that way. They haven't told me directly, but they told the President that the system I proposed is too paper heavy and awkward. Three years now seems like an impossible time frame for them to get their heads around. They're telling the President that one year is good enough in the kind of changeable environment we're in now."

"It must feel like all your effort has been wasted." Chip was practising being more empathic.

"That's part of it, I suppose. The real kick is that the President started to panic with this input and promised a revised second draft would be presented at the management meeting in two days."

"That's what happened," Hoot winked knowingly. "What do you really think is going on?"

"I've got this strong feeling that I'm just seeing the tip of the iceberg. I find it hard to believe that the weight of the paper is the real issue. I think there are other concerns that aren't out on the table yet."

"What fascinates me is the President's response. Why such a quick promise to have it all taken care of in two days?" Hoot was still digging for the real message.

"I'm not sure. Maybe he doesn't want the issue to get any bigger than it is."

"Or he thinks the issue is simple and can be thought through in a short time frame," suggested Piggy. "I like his desire to get on with it, but it could be a tad hasty."

Chip turned to The Kid. "Or is he testing you?"

"Or he doesn't have anything else for Friday's agenda." Spit's quip broke the tension in the room.

"We could spend all day trying to second-guess the President's motives, we are dealing with such limited information. Maybe the best thing we can do is get on with our own discussion, given what we do know," Abernathy suggested. Piggy couldn't help but smile to himself. Everybody seemed to be trying to learn from each other. Here was Abernathy pushing to get on with it.

The Kid said he would try to talk with his boss during the day to see if he could get a better fix on his motives for moving so quickly. Being a realist, however, he liked

Abernathy's suggestion of continuing the discussion.

Spit picked up a crayon and started to move to the scribbler. "Here's what we need to do. Record some of the ideas that we've come up with and then restate the issue we're trying to resolve. It'll be a way for us to see where we've been and where we're going."

"Like standing back to see forward," Hoot reflected.

Everyone made eye contact, nodded their approval. Consensus had been reached.

Spit made notes as the group reviewed what had been talked about. A check mark was placed in front of each item. The first points came in a flurry. Spit wrote as quickly as she could.

✓ Top-down planning systems don't respond to the needs of today's employees.

✓ Employees are used to and want involvement, participation, and the feeling that what they contribute is valued.

✓ An organization gains focus by defining what business it is in.

✓ Organizations need leaders who are people literate.

✓ Individuals move in the direction of vision.

Spit tore off a page, posted it with dressmaker pins, and moved on to the next one.

✓ We need to learn to deal with the whole person ... attitudes, skills, and knowledge.

✓ If you're not part of the solution, you are part of the problem.

✓ Anything that has been changed, can be changed.

✓ Things will stay the same, unless they change.

After the initial rush of ideas, the rest came more slowly. Abernathy noted that some of the items were part of Hoot's Observations. Chip commented on self-management and the steps to personal maturity.

There was a feeling of satisfaction. They had discovered a lot together.

Spit now took the crayon and, in large letters, wrote, OUR FOCUS.

The Kid started in, "As I understand it now, the President is really looking for a process that will ensure that the organization *is changed, can change, and can make change.*" Spit printed those words in block letters.

"If that reality is in place," The Kid continued, "the organization can approach the 21st century boldly. He has also said that he wants everybody to think and behave strategically. At some level, he recognizes that it can't be the senior people alone who own the responsibility for change, everybody needs to have their fingerprints on it."

"Our challenge is to think about how to make organizations change ready," Piggy reiterated.

"As long as change ready doesn't imply passively sitting back and waiting for things to happen," The Kid clarified.

"You're right. By change ready I mean 'is changed, can change, and can make change.'" They all recognized the value of being more precise when a deadline was closer. Making sure that everyone was clear about the focus would be a wise investment.

Spit put down the crayon and moved over to lean on the bell of the trombone. Piggy leaned forward, turned to Abernathy and said, "Since our focus is clearly on change, maybe you should share with everybody the three Change Insights that we came up with last night."

Spit and Chip looked at one another, then over at Abernathy, and then back at each other.

"You helped write these?" Spit pressed.

"When we were talking about these this morning, you did not say anything." Chip was bewildered.

"I can't believe you just sat there and let us blather on."

"When you listen, you learn what somebody else knows, when you talk you only repeat what you already know," Abernathy offered. "I was trying to learn."

Spit nodded to Chip, turned to Piggy and offered a mock bow. "We're flattered." Everyone smiled.

Abernathy waddled over to where the Change Insights were posted. He pointed to the first one, "Change is," and commented that change is a natural reality. He built on the growth metaphor that he had heard Chip and Spit develop.

"Go with the flow is what Emily tells me when she thinks I'm too tense or upset," The Kid offered.

"East meets West," Hoot observed.

Abernathy then pointed out that to resist change is energy-depleting and extremely draining. "When you are part of the changing reality you are filled with vitality, excitement, and contentment. When you resist, you feel drained, tired, and ill-at-ease."

Spit and Chip grinned at one another, enjoying the fact that they had understood.

"'Gotta wanna,'" Abernathy was pointing to the second Insight, "speaks to the notion of motivation. No growth, change, or development will happen unless there is a strong internal desire. Those involved in change have to see a benefit of doing things differently."

The Kid wanted to test. "The implication is that there needs to be some feedback system which lets the organization know what other changes are occuring around it and what will happen if the organization continues on its current path. That information should create some desire to move, shift, change, whatever."

"If trend analysis has any value," Spit interjected, "this is it. Trend analysis should tell you what life would look like *if*."

"And the last one," The Kid inquired, "'Inside out?'"

Abernathy deferred to Piggy. "This one caused us the most discussion and we're not absolutely sure we know what it all means."

As Piggy paused, searching for the right words, Abernathy began slowly. "If change is going to be real and honest, the organization has to start at its core. Otherwise, the change won't be authentic, part of its total way of being."

The very words Abernathy used were soft and intangible, difficult to hold. The silence in the meeting begged for more definition. Piggy wasn't sure if further explanation would help, but he decided to give it a run. "Each organization has a distinct culture that defines how it thinks, feels, and acts as well as what it values and holds to be important."

"Corporate culture is to organizations what personality is to individuals?" Chip asked.

"Sort of," Piggy conceded. "Our assumption was that if real change is going to happen in an organization, you have to deal with the nature of the corporate culture, its core ... things like values, traditions, purposes, that sort of stuff."

There must have been some connection. Piggy could see The Kid making mental notes. Chip was whispering to Spit, "We weren't that far off. Dealing with corporate culture is to an organization what self-management is to individuals."

"What I'm beginning to realize," The Kid leaned into the conversation, "is that planning is a small part of change-making. Somebody has to get their mitts on the corporate culture and articulate purpose and vision, define values, spin traditions, if change is going to be made and our future secured."

There was some silent mull time.

Spit took up a position beside Abernathy. "I must admit, it was this last one that had us puzzled, 'The colour of change is grey.' I take it that that was a spoof?"

Before either Abernathy or Piggy could reply, Hoot began speaking slowly and methodically. "There was a time when black was black and white was white. The good guys wore the white hats and the bad guys wore the black hats. The world was defined and put into tight little boxes."

She was gaining momentum. "In this environment, everything was predictable. Then the global village started to form, we became more cosmopolitan, we mixed ideas, cultures, perceptions, values, tools, and techniques. The lines became blurred, fuzzy. Complexity was added when the rate of change started to double and triple. New worlds were created in less than a generation. Now black is no longer black and white is no longer white, there are only greys. Life is the yin and the yang, opposites joined together."

"I like that," Abernathy smiled. "Change is grey," he confirmed.

Hoot continued. "Carl Sandburg once described a paradox as two truths standing on opposite mountains calling each other liars. The truth, of course, is in the valley."

That comment drew furrowed brows from everyone but Piggy. "She's right," he said, vibrating with excitement. "Think about how many organizations try to plan or make change with a black and white mentality. They totally dedicate themselves to efficiency. They exploit that strategy to the 'nth' degree only to discover that they have lost all their customers. Then they swing the pendulum in the other direction and it is efficiency be damned, customer service is now the rallying cry. Why try to resolve the tension in one direction or the other? The truth is in the valley ... friendly efficiency."

Hoot smiled, she liked opening doors.

The Kid pushed one step further. "Change-makers have the obligation to help the organization identify its essential paradox. Once that paradox has been identified, strategy can be shaped and crafted."

Chip had followed everything up to the The Kid's conclusion. "What do you mean when you say 'help an organization identify its essential paradox?' That almost implies that friendly efficiency is not the critical paradox for every organization."

"I don't think it could be the same; organizations can be as varied as individuals." Hoot merely stated the obvious.

"So," Spit said with a twinkle in her eye, "let's have some fun and brainstorm paradoxes. Remember the rule, suspend critical judgement." There were a few half-reluctant looks and then Spit herself started. "Give more with less."

"Mass customization," Hoot offered. She had read that somewhere but couldn't remember the source.

"Exploitive conservation."

"Quality on time."

"Profitable service."

The paradoxes were coming fast and furious, it was unclear who was saying what.

"Limited possibilities."

"Crafted automation."

"Programmed exceptions."

"Centralized freedom."

"Secured risks."

"Independent dependencies."

"You could even apply this idea of paradoxes to departments, to managers, or even to individuals," added Chip. With this they were off in another direction.

"Dream workable solutions."

"Hold on loosely," Piggy offered, then explained, "that's one for managers." The others all looked at him to remind him that justifying a response was not necessary when brainstorming.

"Question answers."

"Stand back to see forward. That's got to be one for us," suggested Abernathy.

"Either that or 'thoughtful action,'" countered Piggy.

"Playful work."

"Challenging repetitions."

"Empowered controls."

"Aggressive compromise."

"Intuitive logic."

They continued until exhausted. No censoring, no evaluating. Brainstorming itself was a paradox, a process of competitive co-operation. One idea pushed you to come up with another, everybody benefited.

Piggy eased himself out of his seat, walked behind it, and stood there, his arms resting on the back. "If an organization could come to grips with the nature of its essential paradox, it would have a cauldron in which to cook strategy."

"Do you think there is only one key paradox or could

there be several?" Hoot queried. No one knew if she had the answer to her own question.

"I'm not absolutely positive. My hunch is that there is usually only one paradox that is central to the nature of the business. Within departments, there may be different ones, depending on the service that they provide to the organization."

Hoot said she thought his hunch was right. "I rather suspect that if an organization tried to deal with more than one paradox as it developed strategy, it would divert itself."

Chip thought the same was true of individuals. "I think that my paradox is to question answers. For too long I have followed old programming, programming that kept me pretty low on the personal maturity ladder."

No one felt the need to comment. Piggy started to make connections. "The definition of what business you are in comes first. Then you can shape strategy from your essential paradox. Strategy should follow from purpose."

Chip's board was lighting up. "Maybe we should all think this one through, our paradoxes I mean, and then test them with each other just like we did with our mission statements."

Abernathy was still back a beat or two. "What a superb metaphor you used, Piggy – a cauldron in which to cook strategy. It suggests blending ideas, boiling them down to the essence ... " He was about to take the metaphor further when they all heard a loud slam.

The Kid's attention was diverted. "It must be Emily going to work. If that's the case, I've got to be going, too. Could we meet tomorrow night? I'm sure I'll have a draft of the report I'm going to present to the Executive Committee by then."

It seemed like an odd ending to a meeting that was just rolling, but they all agreed. "Just after dusk?" Abernathy suggested. All nodded.

Each Gave a Gift 10

THE SUN HAS NOT YET SET, but Abernathy, Chip, and Piggy have already gathered to wait for the others. There is both a sense of anticipation and apprehension in the air, even Abernathy is up on all fours, pacing.

"I thought some more about what business I am in and what my central paradox might be," started Chip. He had the attention of Piggy and Abernathy. "You may recall that I said I was in the business of taking personal responsibility for everything that I undertake so that those around me might do the same."

He got nods.

"The more I thought about it, the more it became clear that the only reason I wanted to take personal responsibility was so that I could make someone else take responsibility for herself. I had fallen into the trap of owning her problem, a violation of one of Hoot's Observations. So I decided to amend my statement to this: I am in the business of taking personal responsibility for everything I undertake."

"If the statement ends there," Piggy reinforced, "you own what legitimately belongs to you and those around you can decide for themselves how they choose to respond to you."

"That is exactly the thought process I went through. I then began to consider what my central paradox might be so that I could shape my strategies and plans, and I think the one I first settled on is right for me: question answers." Chip was confident in his conclusion. "What about the two of you?"

Piggy was ready. If the truth be known, he arrived early so he could have this dialogue. "My 'business' had to do with competency, doing my best. I think the statement is still right for me. My paradox comes from the issue that has plagued me for the better part of my life: thoughtful action. I know I have the ability to be thoughtful, but my desire to get on with things overrides reflection."

Abernathy nodded knowingly, his problem was the reverse. He worried on occasion whether he was too slow to act. Just as Abernathy was going to talk about his paradox, Hoot swooped by and landed on her fishing pole perch. "Let me guess," she said, "you're talking about personal paradoxes that may complement your statements about what business you're in."

Chip wondered how she knew. The more he thought about it, the more he realized that Hoot was only reading patterns, not tea leaves. This is what always happened, individuals arrived early to make personal connections.

Hoot continued, "The paradox which is critical for me is intuitive logic. I have this urge to want to resolve the paradox in favour of logic and I don't always trust my intuition. There is a time and place for gut hunch, especially when you're imagining possibilities."

"But you can always see the patterns, you know where things are headed," Chip declared.

"My feeling is that seeing implications is not the same as intuition, which is more gut hunch," Hoot offered.

"You blaze the trail I'm sure I'll be following some day," Chip smiled.

Spit could be heard whistling "When You Wish Upon a Star" as she made her way past the baby buggy to The Meeting Place. There was a dreamy quality to the way she did it. Everyone in Wasiswill loved the tune, Walt's theme song. It was a real salute to wonder and joy and the man who delivered many toys from the wooden age to the cuddle age.

"Spit must be in love," Abernathy speculated. When she turned the corner past the rocker, she caught the gaze of all of them. The tune vanished and Spit assumed her typical composure. Chip caught himself staring and then blurted, "And what is your paradox Spit?"

Spit paused for the purpose of drama, not because she hadn't considered the question. "Hold on loosely, and yours, Abernathy?" she quickly countered.

"Well, it's aggressive compromise, I guess."

"You're not sure."

"Not absolutely, to be quite honest. I do know that I resolve the paradox – at least I think I resolve it – on the compromise side. Then I feel I've done too much of that and I should be more assertive so right out of the blue I push to have my own way. But everybody knows that that bark has no bite." Abernathy stopped mid-thought. "Maybe my paradox should be constructive confrontation so that when I am at odds with others I am reminded to confront the issue sooner rather than later."

"It sounds like you're still struggling with it," Piggy reflected.

"I am. I also recognize that it's mine to resolve."

As that was being said they all heard footsteps. They rushed to their usual places as The Kid sat down amongst them. They all waited for The Kid to start.

"I'm sorry I rushed out the last time, but I still haven't given myself permission to be late for work or even to take a mental health day."

"Not all habits are bad," Hoot offered.

"I also have the feeling that what I've prepared isn't complete and I should do some more work on it before I present it to you."

"C'mon Kid, stop should-ing yourself. Give what you've got." Spit had no patience for the apology dance.

"In putting my proposal together –" this was just like doing a dry run for the management committee "– I have tried to respect several notions. First –" he grabbed his index finger "– I have attempted to make the process highly involving and participative. That both respects the needs of today's employees and also ensures that the corporate agenda to have 'everyone thinking and behaving strategicially' is met."

"Wise move." That was an expected response from Hoot.

"Second." The Kid was gathering strength of conviction as he went. It was odd how he felt jitters making a presentation like this in front of old friends. "I have used the planning methodology as only one part of the total change-making process. I recognize that planning and change are not the same thing. Planning is one of many methodologies to help change, or to use our term, making the organization change ready."

"A victory for dialogue," punctuated Piggy. He was looking very comfortable in his wingback.

"The third notion. Leadership and management join together in the process. One set of attitudes, skills, and knowledges is not better than another. We need to have vision and people literacy coupled with controls that set and monitor the use of resources. We need both."

Spit shifted from foot to foot, looking like she wanted to argue, then held her tongue and nodded. The Kid was right. It isn't either/or, it is both/and. "This is the nature of paradox." Spit was beginning to understand. "When faced with two equally difficult choices, I choose both. You have gone the path of controlled vision."

"Perhaps you're right," The Kid continued. "Fourth, I have tried to respect the intent and direction of the Wasiswill Code and Hoot's Seven Observations. These are the benchmarks of personal and corporate responsibility and they establish sound principles with respect to making change."

"How can we argue with those notions? They are the product of our discussion and dialogue," Abernathy summarized. Everyone nodded.

"Now you all remember the challenge that the President left with me." The Kid pointed to the posted page from the day before: "'Ensure the organization *is changed, can change, and can make change.*' That is my focus. The decision I made, when mapping out a course of action to achieve that purpose, was to start at the cultural core. That core has five ingredients."

Spit knew another list was coming. She counted on her fingers. "One."

"Purpose. This is the definition of what business you're in. Our discussion of the other day proves the value of resolving that question."

"Two."

"Values. These are the moral benchmarks by which any organization operates. They declare to everyone what the organization stands for."

"Three."

"Traditions. This is a definition of all the things that we carry from the past that are useful in telling others who we are and what we stand for."

"Four."

"Strategies. This is the definition of how purpose will be pursued and is crafted by coming to grips with the essential paradox of the organization."

"And five?" Spit lead The Kid.

"Plans. This is the exact description of how resources will be spent, what energy will be dedicated and what programs will be initiated. A plan defines who is going to do what by when, what support is required, and what the anticipated costs are."

Spit was about to go to the other hand for six but The Kid shook his head. "I've come to the realization that organizations are not full democracies, we can't all get into the marketsquare and stamp our spears. So purpose, values, traditions, and strategies are owned by the senior level. This is a leadership function. That doesn't mean that everybody can't have some input. In fact, I'm suggesting Town Meetings be held during which bottom-up input is gathered and conflicting positions are argued."

"But when push comes to shove," Piggy clarified, "it is the senior people who have to call it?"

"Yes. If you own it, it is yours to call."

Piggy liked that.

"Plans are moulded by everybody who has the ability to spend and invest any of the organization's resources, be it time, energy, money, talent."

"That really means everybody, then," Chip noted, "because even the person who rolls a piece of paper into a printer is investing their wage in that activity."

"I came to the same conclusion. The planning function I had the senior level doing needs to be driven down to the lowest possible, reasonable level, which means everybody plans. Management's job in the planning process is to monitor actual to reality, to coach, to train – those are still useful functions.

"But here's an interesting twist," The Kid went on. "I'm going to suggest that every department see itself as a smaller company within a larger conglomerate and go through the same process of defining what business it is in, as well as developing key strategies."

"One should complement the other, of course," Hoot was quick to add.

"Of course."

Abernathy's tail began to thump, a sure sign that he was excited. "You said that values were the moral benchmarks by which an organization operates." The Kid nodded. "I once heard values described as the 'shoulds' and 'oughts' of our actions, our constants. When I think of values, I think of integrity, honesty, fiscal prudence, respect for differences, working hard, equality … "

"Fairness, innovation, achievement," Piggy added.

"Openness, loyalty," Spit offered in counterpoint.

"You've got it," The Kid said. He turned to Abernathy, "I came to the same conclusions about values. They are the constants when purpose, strategies, and plans are changing."

Wasiswill was a community built on values, whether it had written them down or not. The Code was the closest that it had come to articulating a values statement. "Wouldn't it be a wise idea for any organization to make its value system explicit, Wasiswill included?" Hoot was asking a rhetorical question. "Then we could all understand the boundaries. When boundary definitions are explicit, there is so much more freedom to act and you don't have to guess what is in-bounds and out-of-bounds behaviour."

They spent the next few minutes talking about what

some of their values statements might be. They were beginning to discover that so much of what they were talking about applied not only to The Kid's organization but also to them. The journey out is a journey in.

Chip was buzzing with excitement. "I think I'm going to take your model," he said turning to The Kid, "and use it to get my own thinking straight." Everybody waited for more. Chip wasn't sure what else could be said. He started cautiously, feeling his way. Chip was using whatever intuition he had. "Suppose I were to think of myself as a corporation."

Imagine, Hoot thought to herself, Chip is doing non-linear thinking.

"What kind of corporation?" Piggy asked.

"It really doesn't matter." Chip was rapid processing. "I'll call it Self Corp. If I follow The Kid's format, the statement I made about the business I'm in is like a statement of purpose. The second component is values, the moral benchmarks. If I worked out a clear statement of what my values were, I'd have a personal credo which would define how to live, what to do and how to be."

"Let me guess what a personal credo might sound like." Hoot established her gaze to the top rafter to help her focus. "I respect the worth and independence of individuals and believe that each is capable of magnificient contribution. I will be fair and honest in my relationships with others and trust to the limit of my heart."

Spit smiled, she liked it. She turned to Chip. "Would you do the same thing with traditions?"

"I'm not sure," Chip admitted. "In an organization, traditions are communicated in stories told in speeches by senior executives and in newsletters."

"A journal, diary, photo album, or even an attic

could be the best statement of traditions," Abernathy offered.

"We've already talked about strategies," Chip continued, "the last component is plans. It seems to me that Self Corp. should set goals, objectives, and plans in several departments … career, social, family, intellectual, emotional, and spiritual."

"Of course," Piggy interjected, "your strategy statement should shape your plans." Chip consented. "But don't make them so fat," Piggy went on "and complicated," he was making the point slowly for emphasis, "that you are overwhelmed and fail to implement the plan."

"My feeling is that you would want to develop the plan in conjunction with others," Abernathy pointed out. "If they are affected, they should be part of the discussion."

"Point heard." Hoot nodded in the direction of both Piggy and Abernathy. She then shifted feet as she shifted subjects. She wondered out loud whether organizations were really unique or merely different by degree. As soon as she had made that statement she quickly came to the conclusion that they only differed by degree.

"Our similarity gives us reason to hope." Spit was very definite about this. "If we were unique there would be no hope for any of us because we wouldn't know how to respond. The last thing in the world anybody wants is a unique disease because we don't know what to do when that new disease occurs. I'd rather get a garden variety cold that a doctor has treated 20,000 times than a disease nobody has ever seen before."

Abernathy was feeling uncomfortable with this. He had often made speeches about how every person is special. Spit, sensing this, turned to Abernathy. "That doesn't mean that we aren't special. What makes us special is the specific combinations of purpose, values, traditions, and actions ... and the worth that each of us has inherently." The wagging resumed.

Spit then turned her attention to The Kid. "I like the traditions component that you've added. My hunch is that traditions are not passed on in formal documents as much as they are communicated by story, riddle, nickname, and anecdote. Tradition stories create a useable past so that a useable future can be built."

"We grow from our roots." Vintage Abernathy.

Chip had been listening to the discussion without saying much. He heard the praise for the format that The Kid was suggesting and he listened to the ideas it was built on. The group became aware of Chip's recent silence.

"What's happening with you?" Abernathy prompted.

"I've just been doing a lot of thinking, different thinking than I've done in the past. This is thinking that looks at consequence and implications. It is probably the next generation for me." Everybody smiled.

"I've come to the conclusion that the closer the future is to us, the less ability we have to see what is coming. If change is happening so quickly, it may be impossible to see forward with any perspective at all. The easiest thing is to view life through a rearview mirror and use a 'was' solution in an 'is' situation, or even come to the conclusion that since the future is so unclear, we should just try anything. The wisest thing to do is to stand back to see forward."

Chip turned to The Kid and they connected, eye to eye. "If you think that your senior people might be tempted to do the easiest thing, take them to an environment where you can increase the chances that they will do the wisest thing. When thinking about the tough issues of change, it is so easy to get distracted by what is hurting you today."

"'Will' is often blinded by the tyrannical urgency of the 'is,'" Hoot confirmed.

The dialogue then moved to the challenge The Kid could have ahead of him as he worked with the organization in defining purpose, values, strategies, and traditions. Each of the ingredients, they concluded, was as important as any other. Chip pointed out that the plan should be re-evaluated frequently and modified as necessary. Piggy liked that idea because it responded to his concern about maintaining flexibility.

The night was long ... the feeling in Wasiswill was good ... differences diminished ... they moved to touch, they connected.

"We must leave and make you an orphan again," Hoot finally said. Everyone knew that this meeting must end and that The Kid was on his own to make it happen. One of the values of The Meeting Place was that it always forced you out, pushed you to action.

A sweet sadness filled Wasiswill. Abernathy wished they could meet more often to talk like this. At the same time, he knew that it was best to touch when it was important.

He and Piggy moved now to post their Change Insights beside the Wasiswill Code, the P.S. was now number four. Hoot did the same with her Seven Observations. Chip detached himself from his joystick. Spit thanked the group, somewhat uncharacteristically, for the engagement. Hoot wiped a tear.

Each had given a gift.

The Wasiswill Code

1. *The person who spills the milk, cleans it up.*

2. *The walls we build to keep others out also keep us in.*

3. *What we fear most, we should face first.*

4. *Be care-full.*

Hoot's Observations

1. *What you give is what you get.*

2. *Help yourself.*

3. *The best way to change somebody else is to change yourself.*

4. *There are never mistakes, only lessons.*

5. *Things will stay the same unless they change.*

6. *You can't help a person who doesn't have a problem.*

7. *Anything that has been changed, can be changed.*

Change Insights

1. *Change is.*

2. *Gotta wanna.*

3. *Inside out.*

4. *The colour of change is grey.*

CHANGE IS.

Who do you know who is facing a change and could benefit from *Change Is.*, a useful personal guide for understanding and making change?

Please send me _____ copies of *Change Is.* at $25.95 each, including shipping. GST extra.

Full Name: _____

Address: _____

_____

City: _____

Province: _____ Postal Code: _____

Telephone Numbers: _____

For an order of ten or more books, we offer a discount. There are three easy ways to communicate with us.

1 Call us at (519) 664-1333

2 Fax us at (519) 664-1334

3 Write to us: Charles Nathan Publishing
46 King Street South
St. Jacobs, Ontario
Canada N0B 2N0

BILLING INFORMATION

☐ Cheque is enclosed for total order
☐ Purchase order is attached
☐ Credit Card purchase as designated below
    ☐ Visa   ☐ American Express   ☐ Mastercard

Account No.: _____ Expiration Date: _____

Authorizing Signature: _____

CHANGE IS.

Who do you know who is facing a change and could benefit from *Change Is.*, a useful personal guide for understanding and making change?

Please send me _____ copies of *Change Is.* at $25.95 each, including shipping. GST extra.

Full Name: _____

Address: _____

_____

City: _____

Province: _____ Postal Code: _____

Telephone Numbers:_____

For an order of ten or more books, we offer a discount. There are three easy ways to communicate with us.

1 Call us at (519) 664-1333

2 Fax us at (519) 664-1334

3 Write to us: Charles Nathan Publishing
46 King Street South
St. Jacobs, Ontario
Canada N0B 2N0

BILLING INFORMATION

☐ Cheque is enclosed for total order
☐ Purchase order is attached
☐ Credit Card purchase as designated below
   ☐ Visa   ☐ American Express   ☐ Mastercard

Account No.: _____ Expiration Date: _____

Authorizing Signature:_____

CHANGE IS.

Who do you know who is facing a change and could benefit from *Change Is.*, a useful personal guide for understanding and making change?

Please send me _____ copies of *Change Is.* at $25.95 each, including shipping. GST extra.

Full Name: _____

Address: _____

_____

City: _____

Province: _____ Postal Code: _____

Telephone Numbers:_____

For an order of ten or more books, we offer a discount. There are three easy ways to communicate with us.

1 Call us at (519) 664-1333

2 Fax us at (519) 664-1334

3 Write to us: Charles Nathan Publishing
46 King Street South
St. Jacobs, Ontario
Canada N0B 2N0

BILLING INFORMATION

☐ Cheque is enclosed for total order
☐ Purchase order is attached
☐ Credit Card purchase as designated below
  ☐ Visa   ☐ American Express   ☐ Mastercard

  Account No.: _____ Expiration Date:_____

  Authorizing Signature:_____